teach yourself®

better bridge

better bridge
david bird

For over 60 years, more than 50 million people have learnt over 750 subjects the **teach yourself** way, with impressive results.

be where you want to be
with **teach yourself**

For UK order enquiries: please contact Bookpoint Ltd, 130 Milton Park, Abingdon, Oxon, OX14 4SB. Telephone: +44 (0) 1235 827720. Fax: +44 (0) 1235 400454. Lines are open 09.00–17.00, Monday to Saturday, with a 24-hour message answering service. Details about our titles and how to order are available at www.teachyourself.co.uk

For USA order enquiries: please contact McGraw-Hill Customer Services, PO Box 545, Blacklick, OH 43004-0545, USA. Telephone: 1-800-722-4726. Fax: 1-614-755-5645.

For Canada order enquiries: please contact McGraw-Hill Ryerson Ltd, 300 Water St, Whitby, Ontario, L1N 9B6, Canada. Telephone: 905 430 5000. Fax: 905 430 5020.

Long renowned as the authoritative source for self-guided learning – with more than 50 million copies sold worldwide – the **teach yourself** series includes over 500 titles in the fields of languages, crafts, hobbies, business, computing and education.

British Library Cataloguing in Publication Data: a catalogue record for this title is available from the British Library.

Library of Congress Catalog Card Number: on file.

First published in UK 2006 by Hodder Education, 338 Euston Road, London, NW1 3BH.

First published in US 2006 by The McGraw-Hill Companies, Inc.

This edition published 2006.

The **teach yourself** name is a registered trade mark of Hodder Headline.

Typeset by Transet Limited, Coventry, England.
Printed in Great Britain for Hodder Education, a division of Hodder Headline, an Hachette Livre UK Company, 338 Euston Road, London, NW1 3BH, by Cox & Wyman Ltd, Reading, Berkshire.

The publisher has used its best endeavours to ensure that the URLs for external websites referred to in this book are correct and active at the time of going to press. However, the publisher and the author have no responsibility for the websites and can make no guarantee that a site will remain live or that the content will remain relevant, decent or appropriate.

Hodder Headline's policy is to use papers that are natural, renewable and recyclable products and made from wood grown in sustainable forests. The logging and manufacturing processes are expected to conform to the environmental regulations of the country of origin.

Impression number   10 9 8 7 6 5 4 3 2
Year   2010 2009 2008 2007

contents

foreword

The accompanying volume, *Teach Yourself Bridge*, covered the basics of the game. All the opening bids were described and how you should respond to them. There were further chapters on the opener's rebid and responder's rebid. In the section on slam bidding, the cue-bidding of controls and basic Blackwood were covered. The two chapters on defensive bidding addressed take-out and penalty doubles, also the various types of overcall and how to respond to them. The sections on dummy play described some of the techniques required for both suit and no-trump contracts. The basic moves in defence, including opening leads and signals, were also covered.

So, what areas will be tackled in this new book, *Teach Yourself Better Bridge*? We will look at the most popular bidding conventions used in tournament bridge, where players strive to the utmost to bid their own cards accurately and to disrupt the opponents' auction. We will see many of the most important ways to play the dummy, including elimination play, the cross-ruff, dummy reversal, communications play, safety plays and counting the hand. Finally, we will look more closely at defence, in particular at communications, promoting trump tricks and holding up high cards. Absorb all the advice and you will achieve every bridge fanatic's aim – to become a better player. Good luck!

David Bird

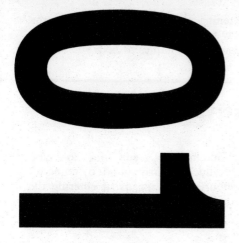

01

preserving declarer's communications

In this chapter you will learn:
- how to duck to preserve an entry to dummy
- how to duck to guard against a bad break
- how to duck twice in a suit
- how to use the trump suit for entries
- how to win the opening lead in the right hand.

Nothing is more disheartening than to see winners in the dummy but to have no way to reach them. In this chapter we will look at the most important techniques to help you stay in touch with the dummy.

Ducking to preserve an honour as an entry

When you are setting up dummy's long suit in a no-trump contract, is often beneficial to duck an early round. By doing so, you preserve dummy's honour(s) as a means of entering the dummy later. Look at the diamond suit on this deal:

```
                    ♠ A
                    ♥ 5 4
                    ♦ A K 9 7 5 2
                    ♣ J 7 6 4
   ♠ Q J 10 6 4        ┌─────────┐       ♠ 8 5 3 2
   ♥ Q 9               │    N    │       ♥ K 10 7
   ♦ J 10 6            │ W     E │       ♦ Q 4
   ♣ Q 8 2             │    S    │       ♣ K 9 5 3
                       └─────────┘
                    ♠ K 9 7
                    ♥ A J 8 6 3 2
                    ♦ 8 3
                    ♣ A 10
```

West	North	East	South
–	–	–	1♥
Pass	2♦	Pass	2♥
Pass	3♣	Pass	3NT
End			

West leads the ♠Q against 3NT. How can you make nine tricks?

You have six tricks on top and must seek three more tricks from one of the red suits. Setting up the hearts is no good because you would probably have to give up two tricks in the process and would then lose two hearts and three spades. You would 'lose the race'.

A better idea is to establish dummy's diamonds. Provided the defenders' cards in the suit divide 3–2, you can set up the three extra winners you need by surrendering the lead just once. How should the play go?

Suppose you play the ace and king of diamonds, both defenders following, and then lead a third round of diamonds to West's jack. You will have three diamond winners in dummy, yes, but they will be stranded. There will be no way to reach them. A better idea is to lead a low diamond from dummy at Trick 2, allowing the defenders to win the first round of the suit. Do you see the point of this? When you regain the lead you can cross to the ♦A, cash the ♦K and score five diamond tricks. In other words, you will have an entry to the diamond winners in dummy.

Ducking to guard against a bad break

On the last deal it was clear that you would have to lose a round of diamonds, even if the defenders' cards divided 3–2, the most favourable break possible. Sometimes you duck an early round of dummy's long suit, just in case it breaks badly. Look at this deal:

```
                    ♠ 8 7 5
                    ♥ 6 3
                    ♦ 9 6
                    ♣ A K Q 8 7 2
    ♠ K J 3                             ♠ Q 9 4
    ♥ Q 9 7 4        ┌─────────┐        ♥ K 8 2
    ♦ Q J 10 5 2     │    N    │        ♦ 8 7 3
    ♣ 9              │  W   E  │        ♣ J 10 5 3
                     │    S    │
                     └─────────┘
                    ♠ A 10 6 2
                    ♥ A J 10 5
                    ♦ A K 4
                    ♣ 6 4
```

West	North	East	South
–	–	–	1NT (15–17)
Pass	3NT	End	

West leads the ♦Q against 3NT. You have seven top tricks and need two more tricks to make the contract. If the defenders' clubs break 3–2, you can simply play the suit from the top (beginning with the ace, king and queen). The remaining three cards will then be good and you will score an overtrick.

What will happen if you follow this line and the defenders' clubs break 4–1, as in the diagram? You will go down! You could establish two extra winners in clubs, by giving up a club trick, but you would have no way to reach them. Since you need only five club tricks to bring your total to nine, you should duck the first round of clubs. In other words, after winning the diamond lead you play a low club from both hands.

You win the defenders' return and cross to dummy with a club to the ace. The king and queen will draw East's remaining clubs and the ♣8-7 will bring your total to nine tricks. This is an example of a 'safety play', a play that you make to guard against a bad break in a suit. If clubs had broken 3–2, the safety play would have cost you an overtrick, since you would make five club tricks instead of the six that were available. However, this is a small premium to pay to ensure that you make the contract whenever the clubs are 4–1.

Ducking twice in a suit

Sometimes you have to duck twice in a suit, preserving dummy's ace as an entry on the third round. Look at the diamond suit on the next deal:

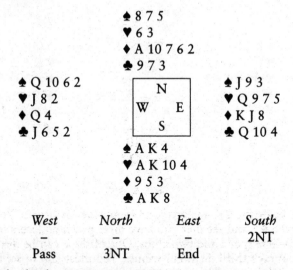

```
                    ♠ 8 7 5
                    ♥ 6 3
                    ♦ A 10 7 6 2
                    ♣ 9 7 3
    ♠ Q 10 6 2          N          ♠ J 9 3
    ♥ J 8 2                        ♥ Q 9 7 5
    ♦ Q 4         W        E       ♦ K J 8
    ♣ J 6 5 2          S          ♣ Q 10 4
                    ♠ A K 4
                    ♥ A K 10 4
                    ♦ 9 5 3
                    ♣ A K 8
```

West	North	East	South
–	–	–	2NT
Pass	3NT	End	

West leads the ♠2 against 3NT. You can count seven top winners and will need to establish two more tricks from dummy's diamond suit. This can be done, provided the defenders' diamonds divide 3–2, but you will need an entry to dummy to reach the two long diamonds. The entry can only be the ♦A, so you must play low on the first two rounds of the suit. How does the play go?

You win East's ♠J with the ♠A and play a low diamond from both hands. East wins the diamond trick and returns another spade. You win with the ♠K and, once again, play a low diamond from both hands. The defenders win the trick and cash two spade tricks. (You knew they would have only two spades to cash because West's fourth-best lead of the ♠2 showed that he held a four-card suit.) When you regain the lead, you cross to the ♦A on the third round of the suit. The lead will then be in dummy – just where you want it! You cash the 10 and 7 of diamonds and that brings your total to nine.

Using the trump suit for entries

The contracts we have seen so far have all been played in no-trumps. Playing with a trump suit may affect matters in two ways: you can establish a side suit by taking ruffs in that suit; you can also use the trump suit to gain entry to the established winners. Let's see a deal where both of those aspects come into play.

```
                    ♠ 8 6
                    ♥ K 7 4
                    ♦ A K Q 7 2
                    ♣ 8 6 3
    ♠ K Q J 3                      ♠ 9 7 5 4 2
    ♥ 10 9 5      ┌─────────┐      ♥ 8 3
    ♦ 10 5        │   N     │      ♦ J 8 6 4
    ♣ Q 10 7 5    │ W   E   │      ♣ J 2
                  │   S     │
                  └─────────┘
                    ♠ A 10
                    ♥ A Q J 6 2
                    ♦ 9 3
                    ♣ A K 9 4
```

West leads the ♠K against your small slam in hearts. You win with the ♠A and see that you have three potential losers in your hand – one spade and two clubs. One of these can be discarded on dummy's third diamond winner. You must aim to set up the diamond suit, so that you can discard another of your three initial losers. How can this be done?

Provided diamonds break no worse than 4–2, you can establish the suit with one ruff. The only entry back to dummy, however, will be the king of trumps. So, you cannot afford to draw all the trumps before setting up the diamond suit. After winning the first trick with the ♠A, you should draw two rounds of trumps with the ace and queen. When trumps break 3–2, you leave the last trump out and play the ace and king of diamonds, both defenders following suit. In case diamonds are breaking 4–2, you next ruff a diamond in your hand. You take this ruff with the ♥J, to make sure that West cannot overruff. You then return to dummy with a trump to the king, drawing West's last trump. You can then cash the ♦Q and ♦7, throwing two of your three black-suit losers. Slam made!

Winning the opening lead in the right hand

When you hold the ace and the king in the suit that has been led, it is sometimes important to win the first trick in the right hand. Usually it is right to preserve an entry to the weaker of the two hands. Would you have made 3NT on this deal?

```
                    ♠ A 5
                    ♥ A K 7 4
                    ♦ A K 8 4
                    ♣ J 5 2
  ♠ Q 9 8 6 2              ♠ J 7 3
  ♥ 8 6 2          N        ♥ Q J 10 9 5
  ♦ J 10 6 2    W     E     ♦ Q 9
  ♣ 4             S         ♣ A 8 3
                    ♠ K 10 4
                    ♥ 3
                    ♦ 7 5 3
                    ♣ K Q 10 9 7 6
```

West	North	East	South
–	1♦	Pass	1NT
Pass	3NT	End	

West leads the ♠6 against your contract of 3NT. How will you plan the play?

Suppose you give the matter little thought and play low from dummy, winning East's ♠J with the ♠K. When you play on clubs, East will hold up his ♣A until the third round of the suit. With no entry left to the South hand, you will score only two club tricks. Two tricks in each suit give you a total of eight and, with the diamond suit not breaking 3–3, you will have no way to increase this to nine. One down.

The old maxim, 'plan the contract before playing to Trick 1' is sound advice! Here you start with six top tricks and can easily set up another five tricks in the club suit. In case the defenders can hold up the ♣A for two rounds, you must make sure that you have an entry to your eventual club winners. So, win the opening lead with dummy's ♠A and play on the club suit. East will doubtless hold up the ♣A for two rounds but it will do him no good. Whether or not he then returns a spade, you will be able to reach your hand with the ♠K to score the three established club tricks. Winning the opening lead in the right hand makes the difference between going one down and scoring two overtricks.

Points to remember

- It is often beneficial to duck an early round (or two) of a suit that you hope to establish. By doing so, you retain the top honour as an entry card.
- When you are in a suit contract and hope to establish a side suit in the dummy, it is often necessary to use entries provided by the trump suit. In such a situation you may have to delay drawing trumps. You plan to establish the side suit and then to 'draw trumps, ending in the dummy'.
- Particularly when you are playing in no-trumps, it can be important to win the opening lead in the right hand. In general, you will want to retain the entry to the hand that began with fewer entries.

Test yourself

(1)

    ♠ A 3 2
    ♥ 8 3
    ♦ J 7 3
    ♣ A K 9 6 4

♥Q led

```
        N
    W       E
        S
```

    ♠ K Q J 10 6 5
    ♥ A K
    ♦ A 6 2
    ♣ 5 2

West	North	East	South
–	1♣	Pass	1♠
Pass	2♣	Pass	4NT
Pass	5♥	Pass	6♠
End			

West leads the ♥Q. How will you plan the play?

(2)

    ♠ A 6 2
    ♥ A 10
    ♦ A 10 8 6 3
    ♣ 8 5 3

♣Q led

```
        N
    W       E
        S
```

    ♠ K 5 4
    ♥ K Q J 9 7 3
    ♦ 9
    ♣ A K 2

West	North	East	South
–	1♦	Pass	1♥
Pass	1NT (12–14)	Pass	3♥
Pass	4♥	Pass	4NT
Pass	5♣	Pass	6♥
End			

West leads the ♣Q against 6♥. How will you play the contract?

Answers

(1)

```
                      ♠ A 3 2
                      ♥ 8 3
                      ♦ J 7 3
                      ♣ A K 9 6 4
     ♠ 8                              ♠ 9 7 4
     ♥ Q J 10 7 5        N            ♥ 9 6 4 2
     ♦ K 10 8 5 4    W       E        ♦ Q 9
     ♣ J 7              S             ♣ Q 10 8 3
                      ♠ K Q J 10 6 5
                      ♥ A K
                      ♦ A 6 2
                      ♣ 5 2
```

West	North	East	South
–	1♣	Pass	1♠
Pass	2♠	Pass	4NT
Pass	5♥	Pass	6♠
End			

West leads the ♥Q against your small slam in spades. How will you plan the play?

You have two losers in diamonds and must hope to establish dummy's clubs, in order to provide one or more discards. If your play in clubs is to cash the ace-king and then to ruff the third round, you will make the slam only when clubs break 3–3.

A better line allows you to succeed against a 4–2 club break. Win the heart lead and draw just one round of trumps with the king. Now lead a club and duck in the dummy! You win the red-suit return and draw a second round of trumps with the queen. Leaving one trump out for the moment, you cross to the ♣A and ruff a club with the ♠J. The club suit is now established – dummy has ♣A-9 left and East holds the bare ♣Q. You return to dummy with the ♠A, drawing East's last trump, and play the two good clubs, throwing both of your diamond losers.

Do you see that it would be a mistake to draw a second round of trumps (with the ♠Q) before ducking a club? When East won the ducked club, he could return a third round of trumps. This would remove the entry to dummy before you had established the club suit.

(2)

```
                              ♠ A 6 2
                              ♥ A 10
                              ♦ A 10 8 6 3
                              ♣ 8 5 3

    ♠ J 8 7              ┌─────────────┐         ♠ Q 10 9 3
    ♥ 6 4 2              │      N      │         ♥ 8 5
    ♦ J 5 2              │  W       E  │         ♦ K Q 7 4
    ♣ Q J 10 7           │      S      │         ♣ 9 6 4
                         └─────────────┘
                              ♠ K 5 4
                              ♥ K Q J 9 7 3
                              ♦ 9
                              ♣ A K 2
```

West	North	East	South
–	1♦	Pass	1♥
Pass	1NT	Pass	3♥
Pass	4♥	Pass	4NT
Pass	5♣	Pass	6♥
End			

South's 4NT is Roman Key-card Blackwood (see Chapter 2) and the 5♣ response shows three or zero aces. West leads the ♣Q against your small slam in hearts. How will you play the contract?

You need to set up dummy's diamond suit, so you can discard one of your black-suit losers. To achieve this, you will need to use both of dummy's entries in the trump suit. Win the club lead and play a diamond to the ace immediately. Ruff a diamond and return to dummy with the ♥10. When you ruff another diamond, you are pleased to see the suit break 4–3. You return to dummy with the ♥A and ruff yet another diamond, establishing a winner in the suit. You draw the last trump and cross to the ♠A. You can then discard a spade or a club on the thirteenth diamond, making your slam.

As it happens, a trump lead would beat the slam. It would remove an entry to the dummy prematurely, before you were able to make use of it.

02

roman key-card blackwood

In this chapter you will learn:
- how to discover how many aces partner holds
- how to discover whether partner holds the king and queen of trumps
- how to discover which side-suit kings partner holds.

The days when 4NT (Blackwood) simply asked how many aces partner held are long since gone. It is recognized nowadays that the king and queen of trumps are equally important cards. So, nearly all tournament players use a 4NT enquiry called Roman Key-card Blackwood (RKCB). The initial responses are based on the five so-called 'key cards', the four aces and the king of trumps.

When a trump suit has been agreed and partner bids 4NT to ask how many key cards you hold, these are the responses:

Roman Key-card Blackwood responses

5♣	0 or 3 key cards
5♦	1 or 4 key cards
5♥	2 or 5 key cards without the queen of trumps
5♠	2 or 5 key cards with the queen of trumps

Suppose you bid 4NT and partner responds 5♣. Nearly always you can tell from partner's previous bidding whether he will hold 0 or 3 key cards. In the occasional situations where you cannot be sure, you temporarily assume that he has no key cards and sign off. When he instead holds 3 key cards, he will make another bid.

Let's see an example of RKCB in action.

West	East	West	East
♠ A K Q 9 3 2	♠ 7 4	1♠	2♥
♥ Q 9 7 2	♥ A K J 8 3	4NT	5♥
♦ A K	♦ 10 7 5	6♥	
♣ 7	♣ Q 10 3		

When West hears a 2♥ response he knows there are only three possible losers in his hand; the defenders might score tricks with the ace and king of trumps and the ace of clubs. He bids a RKCB 4NT to discover how many key cards East holds. The 5♥ response shows two key cards and West therefore bids a small slam, since one trick is likely to be lost to the key card held by the defenders.

If East had shown three key cards, via a 5♣ response, West would have bid a grand slam. If, instead, East had shown only one key card, with a 5♦ response, West would have stopped at the safe level of 5♥. Note that West had a perfect hand for using RKCB. The moment he heard partner's response to 4NT, he would know what contract to choose.

Let's see an example that illustrates the use of the 5♥ and 5♠ responses, which indicate whether the trump queen is held.

West	East	West	East
♠ A J 9 3	♠ K 4	1♣	1♦
♥ A Q 9 7	♥ K J 8 3	1♥	4NT
♦ 5	♦ A K Q 10 7 2	5♠	6♥
♣ Q J 9 7	♣ 3		

West's 5♠ response shows two key cards (which must be aces here) and the ♥Q. One key card is missing and there is a good chance that this will be the only loser. Note that slam bidding is rarely 100 per cent precise. If West's missing key card was ♠A, there might possibly be two spade losers after a spade lead. However, West might hold the ♠Q or the ♠J, which would lessen the chance of two spade losers. Failing that, the ♠A might be with North or North might fail to lead the suit.

Asking for the queen of trumps

We have already seen that possession of the queen of trumps is shown immediately only when the responder has two (or five) key cards. How can the 4NT bidder check on the trump queen when partner holds a different number of key cards?

> When the 4NT bidder continues with the cheapest non-trump bid, he asks for the queen of trumps. Without the trump queen, partner signs off in the trump suit. With the trump queen, he cue-bids his lowest side-suit king, otherwise bids 5NT.

Let's see an example of this:

West	East	West	East
♠ A 9	♠ J 4 2	1♥	3♥
♥ A 10 9 7 3	♥ K Q 8 4	4NT	5♦
♦ A	♦ Q 10 7 2	5♠	6♣
♣ A Q J 9 7	♣ K 4	7♥	

When West hears a double raise in hearts, he can see that the playing strength will be present for a small slam at least. He bids RKCB and hears that partner holds one key card, which must be the ♥K. Already West is happy to play in a small slam. Even if partner holds ♥K-8-5-4 there will be some chance of having no trump loser. If there is a trump loser, the slam may still succeed when East holds the ♣K or the club finesse succeeds.

West is still interested in a grand slam, however. If he bid 5♥ next, this would be a sign-off and partner would pass. West therefore bids 5♠, the cheapest non-trump bid available. This asks East if he holds the queen of trumps. Without the trump queen, East would sign off in 6♥ and West would pass. East actually bids 6♣, which says that not only does he hold the trump queen, he also holds the ♣K. Such a response is music to West's ears! He leaps to 7♥, which will easily be made. If East had bid 5NT, showing the ♥Q but no side-suit king, West would have stopped in 6♥. He would also have stopped at the six-level if East had bid 6♦ to show the ♥Q and the ♦K.

Perhaps you are thinking that this is all a bit complicated. You are right! Still, you can see what an excellent method it is. Instead of guessing whether to bid a slam, you can often be certain whether it is a good idea.

Asking for side-suit kings

Sometimes the response to 4NT tells you that all six important cards (the four aces, the trump king and queen) are held by the partnership. You can then ask for side-suit kings by bidding 5NT. Partner will cue-bid his lowest such king. The following auction arose in the 2005 women's world bridge championship.

West	East	West	East
♠ A K 10 9 2	♠ Q J 8 4 3	1♠	4NT
♥ Q 10 9 7 6 4	♥ A	5♥	5NT
♦ 5	♦ A	6♣	7NT
♣ K	♣ A Q J 10 7 6		

East bid RKCB and found that partner held two key cards, the ace and king of trumps. She continued with 5NT, asking for side-suit kings. With no side-suit kings West would have signed off in 6♠ (returning to the trump suit at the lowest available level). Since West held the ♣K, she responded 6♣ instead. East was now able to count thirteen tricks playing in no-trumps: five spades, two red-suit aces and six clubs. She bid 7NT, which was easily made.

If West had responded 6♥ or 6♦ instead, showing the king of the bid suit, East would have known that there was a potential loser in clubs. She would not have risked bidding a grand slam.

Points to remember

- In tournament play, most players use Roman Key-card Blackwood instead of normal Blackwood. As with any form of Blackwood, a trump suit has to be agreed. The responses to 4NT then show how many key cards are held:

  5♣ 0 or 3 key cards
  5♦ 1 or 4 key cards
  5♥ 2 or 5 key cards without the queen of trumps
  5♠ 2 or 5 key cards with the queen of trumps

- When responder bids 5♣ or 5♦, the 4NT bidder can make the cheapest non-trump bid to ask for the queen of trumps. Responder signs off in the trump suit without the trump queen. Holding the trump queen, he cue-bids his cheapest side-suit king, otherwise bids 5NT.

- When the 4NT bidder knows that the trump queen is held (along with the other five key cards), he can enquire about side-suit kings by bidding 5NT. Partner will then cue-bid his cheapest side-suit king, otherwise sign off in the trump suit.

- It's all a bit complicated, yes, but the extra effort is worth it! You can bid many excellent slams and avoid bidding many poor ones.

Test yourself

(1) The bidding starts like this:

West	North	East	South
1♠	Pass	4NT	Pass
?			

Playing RKCB, what will you bid on the following West hands?

a	♠ A Q 10 8 3	b	♠ K 10 9 7 2	c	♠ J 10 8 6 2
	♥ 9 2		♥ A 8 4		♥ K
	♦ A J 9 3		♦ A 8		♦ A 10 2
	♣ K 4		♣ Q J 4		♣ A K Q 7

(2) The bidding starts like this:

West	North	East	South
1♥	Pass	2♣	Pass
2♥	Pass	4NT	Pass
5♦	Pass	5♠	Pass
?			

Playing RKCB, what will you bid on the following West hands?

a ♠ 6 3   b ♠ K 8 4   c ♠ Q 6
  ♥ A Q 9 8 5 2   ♥ A 10 8 7 3 2   ♥ A Q 8 7 5 2
  ♦ Q J 5   ♦ K Q 5   ♦ Q 8
  ♣ K 6   ♣ 4   ♣ Q 10 2

(3) The bidding starts like this:

West	North	East	South
1♠	Pass	4NT	Pass
5♥	Pass	5NT	Pass
?			

Playing RKCB, what will you bid on the following West hands?

a ♠ A J 9 7 6 2   b ♠ A K J 7 3   c ♠ K J 10 8 7 3
  ♥ A J 8 2   ♥ 4   ♥ K 8 7
  ♦ 5   ♦ Q J 10 4   ♦ A 4
  ♣ K 6   ♣ J 9 3   ♣ K 4

Answers

(1) a **5♠.** Two key cards and the queen of trumps.
   b **5♣.** Three key cards.
   c **5♥.** Two key cards without the queen of trumps.
(2) a **6♣.** 'I do hold the trump queen, also the ♣K.'
   b **6♥.** 'I do not hold the trump queen.'
   c **5NT.** 'I hold the trump queen but no side-suit king.'
(3) a **6♣.** You show the ♣K.
   b **6♠.** With no side-suit king, you sign off in the trump suit.
   c **6♣.** With two side-suit kings, you start by showing the lower king. If partner continues with 6♦, you will have the chance to bid 6♥, showing your other king.

03

promoting trump tricks in defence

The most common way of scoring an extra trump trick in defence is to give partner a ruff. Yes, but you can also promote extra trump tricks in various situations where declarer or the dummy is also void in the side suit being led. The most common way of doing this is to lead a side suit when your partner is in a position to overruff. If declarer chooses to ruff with a high trump, to prevent an overruff, this may create an extra trump winner for the defence. Let's see an example of that.

```
                    ♠ J 10 6 2
                    ♥ Q 5 4 3
                    ♦ A 10 3
                    ♣ K 5
   ♠ Q 4                              ♠ 5
   ♥ 9 7          ┌───────────┐       ♥ A K J 2
   ♦ Q 8 6 2      │    N      │       ♦ J 9 7 5
   ♣ Q 8 7 4 2    │ W     E   │       ♣ J 10 9 6
                  │    S      │
                  └───────────┘
                    ♠ A K 9 8 7 3
                    ♥ 10 8 6
                    ♦ K 4
                    ♣ A 3
```

West	North	East	South
–	–	–	1♠
Pass	3♠	Pass	4♠
End			

Sitting West, you decide to lead the ♥9. This proves to be a lucky choice when East wins with the ♥J. He scores further tricks with the ace and king of hearts and you now need one more trick to beat the contract. Do you see how that trick can be scored?

East continues with the ♥2. What can declarer do? If he ruffs with the ♠9, you will overruff with your ♠Q. If, instead, declarer tries to prevent an overruff by ruffing with the ♠A (or ♠K), your ♠Q will be 'promoted'. What does that mean? It means that its value will be increased so that it subsequently scores a trick. By playing his fourth heart, East achieves what is known as a 'trump promotion'.

Let's see another example of this important technique.

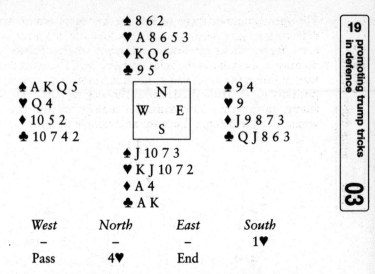

West	North	East	South
–	–	–	1♥
Pass	4♥	End	

Once again you are sitting West. You lead the ♠A and partner encourages a continuation by playing the ♠9. You cash the king and queen of spades successfully, your partner throwing a low diamond on the third round. What now?

You have an excellent chance of a trump promotion if you continue with a fourth round of spades. Look what will happen when the cards lie as in the diagram. If declarer ruffs with dummy's ♥A, to prevent an overruff from East, your ♥Q will become promoted. If, instead, he ruffs with dummy's ♥8, East will overruff with the ♥9. One down either way!

The uppercut

On the two deals we have seen so far, a defender was poised to overruff. You may also be able to promote a trump trick when it is the declarer who will overruff your partner. How can that happen? Your partner ruffs with his highest trump, forcing declarer to overruff with an even higher trump. This may promote the trumps that you hold yourself. Here is a typical example of this spectacular defensive technique.

```
                        ♠ 8 7 6 3
                        ♥ K Q 7
                        ♦ Q 10 6
                        ♣ K J 6
        ♠ Q 5                              ♠ J 4
        ♥ 8 6 4           ┌─────────┐      ♥ A 10 9 2
        ♦ A K 8 7 5 4     │   N     │      ♦ 9 3
        ♣ 7 3          W  │ W     E │  E   ♣ 10 8 5 4 2
                          │   S     │
                          └─────────┘
                        ♠ A K 10 9 2
                        ♥ J 5 3
                        ♦ J 2
                        ♣ A Q 9
```

West	North	East	South
–	–	–	1♠
Pass	3♠	Pass	4♠
End			

Sitting West, you lead the ♦A against South's contract of 4♠. Partner encourages with the ♦9 and you continue with the ♦K, everyone following. There are two good reasons to play another diamond now. Firstly, there is a chance of a trump promotion if East can ruff with the ♠J, forcing a higher trump honour from South. Secondly, you want East to ruff dummy's ♦Q anyway, to stop declarer scoring a trick with it.

When you lead a low diamond on the third round, East cannot be absolutely certain that South has no diamonds left (despite the appearance of the ♦J on the second round). Nevertheless, East has nothing to lose by ruffing high – with the ♠J. As it happens, South has to overruff with the ♠K and West's ♠Q is promoted into a trick. East's ♥A will give the defenders a fourth trick and the contract will go one down.

The technique of ruffing high in defence, knocking a big hole in declarer's trump holding, is known as an 'uppercut'.

When it is wrong to overruff

Suppose you are sitting over the declarer, in a position to overruff the lead that partner has just made. Declarer ruffs with the king and your trump holding is A-10-5. Should you overruff? No! By refusing to overruff, the value of your trump holding will be promoted and you may score a second trump trick. Let's see the situation in the context of a full deal.

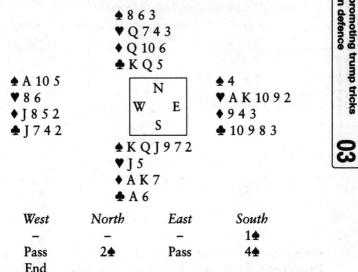

West	North	East	South
–	–	–	1♠
Pass	2♠	Pass	4♠
End			

Sitting West, you lead the ♥8 against South's spade game. Your partner wins with the ♥K and cashes the ♥A. When he continues with the ♥10, declarer ruffs with the ♠K. How should you defend?

If you overruff with the ♠A, the contract will be made! Declarer will win your return and draw your remaining ♠10-5 with his ♠Q-J. Instead, you should refuse to overruff, discarding a diamond or a club. You now hold ♠A-10-5 over South's ♠Q-J-9-7-2. Your trump holding has been promoted and you are certain to score two trump tricks.

Suppose your trumps were slightly weaker: ♠A-9-5. You should still refuse to overruff. This would gain a trick when your partner held the ♠10. Do not overruff when there is any chance that you may promote a second trump trick by discarding instead.

Points to remember

- When partner is in a position to overruff, you can sometimes create an extra trump trick. Declarer will have to ruff high to prevent an overruff and this may promote the defenders' trump holding.

- A second way to promote a trump trick is the 'uppercut'. A defender ruffs with his highest trump, forcing declarer to overruff with an even higher trump.
- Do not overruff a trump honour from a holding such as A-10-5. By discarding instead, you may score a second trump trick with the 10.

Test yourself

(1)

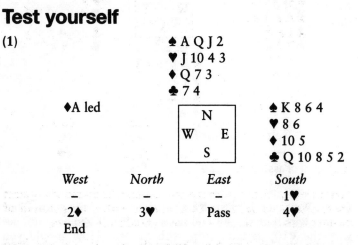

♠ A Q J 2
♥ J 10 4 3
♦ Q 7 3
♣ 7 4

♦A led

♠ K 8 6 4
♥ 8 6
♦ 10 5
♣ Q 10 8 5 2

West	North	East	South
–	–	–	1♥
2♦	3♥	Pass	4♥
End			

Your partner cashes the ♦A, followed by the ♦K. He continues with a third round of diamonds. How should you defend?

(2)

♠ 9 5 3 2
♥ A
♦ K Q 9 4
♣ J 5 3 2

♠ K 10 4
♥ Q J 8 5 2
♦ 6 5 3
♣ 9 6

West	North	East	South
–	–	–	1♠
Pass	3♠	Pass	4♠
End			

You lead the ♣9 against South's contract of 4♠. East wins with the ♣K and cashes the ♣A, the ♣Q falling from South. When East continues with another club, South ruffs with the ♠Q. What is your plan to beat the contract?

Answers

(1)

```
                        ♠ A Q J 2
                        ♥ J 10 4 3
                        ♦ Q 7 3
                        ♣ 7 4
   ♠ 7 5                                    ♠ K 8 6 4
   ♥ Q 9              ┌─────────┐            ♥ 8 6
   ♦ A K J 8 6 2      │   N     │            ♦ 10 5
   ♣ J 6 3            │ W   E   │            ♣ Q 10 8 5 2
                      │   S     │
                      └─────────┘
                        ♠ 10 9 3
                        ♥ A K 7 5 2
                        ♦ 9 4
                        ♣ A K 9
```

West	North	East	South
–	–	–	1♥
2♦	3♥	Pass	4♥
End			

Your partner, West, cashes the ace and king of diamonds against South's heart game. He then continues with a third round of diamonds to dummy's queen. How should you defend?

You should ruff with the ♥8. South may or may not hold another diamond, but it cannot assist you to ruff with the ♥6 instead. Declarer has to overruff your ♥8 with the ♥K and your partner's ♥Q is promoted. That is three tricks for the defence and your ♠K will make it four. One down!

As you see, if you carelessly ruff with the ♥6, declarer will overruff with the ♥7 and draw trumps with the ♥A and ♥K, making the contract.

(2)

```
                        ♠ 9 5 3 2
                        ♥ A
                        ♦ K Q 9 4
                        ♣ J 5 3 2
   ♠ K 10 4                              ♠ 7
   ♥ Q J 8 5 2        ┌─────────┐       ♥ 10 9 6
   ♦ 6 5 3            │    N    │       ♦ J 10 8 2
   ♣ 9 6              │  W   E  │       ♣ A K 10 7 4
                      │    S    │
                      └─────────┘
                        ♠ A Q J 8 6
                        ♥ K 7 4 3
                        ♦ A 7
                        ♣ Q 8
```

West	North	East	South
–	–	–	1♠
Pass	3♠	Pass	4♠
End			

Sitting West, you lead the ♣9 against South's spade game. East wins with the ♣K and cashes the ♣A. He continues with a third round of clubs and declarer ruffs with the ♠Q. How should you defend?

If you overruff, with the ♠K, you will score just one trump trick and the contract will be made. (Declarer will be able to draw your last two trumps with the ♠A-J.) Discard, instead, and all your trumps will move up one notch. You will score both the ♠K and the ♠10 and the contract will go one down.

04

keeping the danger hand off lead

In this chapter you will learn:
- how to finesse into the safe hand
- how to duck into the safe hand
- how to handle a stopper of A-J-x
- when to alter your normal play in a suit
- how to make an avoidance play.

During the play of a hand, particularly in no-trumps, it often happens that one of the defenders becomes 'safe' while the other is 'dangerous'. For example, suppose West leads from a five-card spade suit and you hold up your ♠ A until the third round, exhausting East's spades in the process. West is now the 'danger hand' because if he gains the lead he will cash two spade tricks. East is the 'safe hand' because he has no spades to play. You must therefore aim to develop the play without allowing the danger hand to gain the lead. That is the subject of this chapter.

Finessing into the safe hand

When you have a choice of finesses to take, you will usually want to take the finesse that is into the safe hand. Let's see an example of this technique.

```
               ♠ 5 2
               ♥ A Q 6
               ♦ Q 10 5 3
               ♣ K J 8 3
♠ K Q J 10 4                    ♠ 8 7 3
♥ 8 7 5          N              ♥ K 10 9 4 2
♦ K 7 2       W     E           ♦ 9 6 4
♣ 6 2            S              ♣ 5 4
               ♠ A 9 6
               ♥ J 3
               ♦ A J 8
               ♣ A Q 10 9 7
```

West	North	East	South
–	–	–	1NT (15–17)
Pass	3NT	End	

West leads the ♠K against 3NT. You hold up your ♠A until the third round and East follows all the way. How will you continue?

You have eight top tricks: five club tricks and three aces. You can seek a ninth trick by taking a heart finesse or by taking a diamond finesse. Which is the better idea, do you think?

Suppose you cross to dummy with a club and take a diamond finesse, running the ♦Q. You are taking a finesse into the danger hand. If it loses, West will cash two more spade tricks and the contract will go down. Suppose, instead, that you take a heart finesse, running the ♥J. That finesse will lose too, but you will still make the contract! The heart finesse is into the safe East hand. When East wins with the ♥K he will have no spade to play. He will doubtless switch to a diamond, but you can rise with the ♦A and score nine tricks. Dummy's ♥Q will be your ninth trick.

On that deal you were happy to take a (heart) finesse into the safe hand because even if it lost you would set up an extra trick in the suit. Even when a losing finesse will not set up an extra trick, it can still be right to finesse first into the safe hand. This deal illustrates the situation:

```
                    ♠ 8 4
                    ♥ 6 5
                    ♦ A Q J 10 5
                    ♣ A Q 8 6
 ♠ 10 5 3                              ♠ K J 9 7 2
 ♥ A J 9 4 2        ┌─────────┐       ♥ 10 8 3
 ♦ 7 2             │    N     │       ♦ 8 6 3
 ♣ 5 4 3          W│         │E       ♣ K 2
                   │    S     │
                    └─────────┘
                    ♠ A Q 6
                    ♥ K Q 7
                    ♦ K 9 4
                    ♣ J 10 9 7
```

West	North	East	South
–	–	–	1NT (15–17)
Pass	3NT	End	

West leads the ♥4 against 3NT and you win East's ♥10 with the ♥Q. How will you play the contract?

You have eight tricks on top: five diamonds, two aces and the ♥Q. You could set up the extra trick you need with a successful spade finesse or a successful club finesse. Which finesse should you take first?

East is the danger hand because he is the defender who can lead a heart through your remaining ♥K-7. Suppose you run the ♣J, finessing into the danger hand. If the finesse loses you will go down. East will return a heart and West will score four tricks in the suit. Instead, you should cross to the ♦Q and finesse the ♠Q. You are finessing into the safe hand. As it happens, the finesse will win and you will make the contract. Suppose the finesse had lost, though. West could not continue hearts profitably from his side of the table, and after a diamond or spade continuation you would still have the chance to finesse in clubs. By finessing first into the safe hand you would give yourself two chances instead of just one.

Let's look next at a deal where you have a two-way finesse within a single suit.

```
                        ♠ 9 5
                        ♥ A 7 4
                        ♦ K J 7 3
                        ♣ K 8 5 2
    ♠ K J 7 6 2                          ♠ Q 10 4
    ♥ 8 6 2              N               ♥ J 10 5 3
    ♦ 8 5           W         E          ♦ Q 9 2
    ♣ Q J 3              S               ♣ 10 9 7
                        ♠ A 8 3
                        ♥ K Q 9
                        ♦ A 10 6 4
                        ♣ A 6 4
```

West	North	East	South
–	–	–	1NT (15–17)
Pass	3NT	End	

West leads the ♠6 against 3NT and you hold up your ace until the third round. How will you play the contract?

You have eight top tricks and must develop another trick from one of the minor suits. This is not a very promising proposition in clubs. Even if the suit divided 3–3, and you could set up a long card by conceding a club trick, there is a big risk that it would be West who gained the lead. He might then be able to cash two spade tricks to beat the contract. No, you should look for your ninth trick in the diamond suit. What is the best play in that suit, do you think?

If West holds the ♦Q, a finesse of dummy's ♦J will succeed. If, instead, East holds the ♦Q, a finesse of your ♦10 will win. Which way should you finesse? You will not fall off your chair when you hear that the best idea is to finesse into the safe hand. Here East is the safe hand because in the dangerous situation where spades break 5–3, East will have no spades left.

So, after winning the third round of spades with the ace, you cash the ♦A and play a low diamond to dummy's jack. As it happens, the finesse loses. No matter. East has no spade to play, so you can win his return and score your nine tricks. (If East did hold another spade, the suit would break 4–4 and you would still make the contract.) Make sure you understand why it was right to finesse into the East hand. By doing so, you would make the contract whether or not the diamond finesse won. If, instead, you were to finesse the ♦10 into the danger hand, you would risk going down if the finesse lost.

Ducking into the safe hand

It often happens that you need to duck a round of a suit in order to establish some tricks in it. When one of the defenders is safe and the other dangerous, you will naturally want to duck into the safe hand. Here is a straightforward example of the play:

```
              ♠ K Q 2
              ♥ 8 6 3
              ♦ K 8 4 3
              ♣ K 9 2
♠ J 10 9 4                      ♠ 8 7 3
♥ A 9 4 2        N              ♥ Q J 10 5
♦ 10 9 5      W     E           ♦ Q J 7
♣ J 4            S              ♣ Q 8 7
              ♠ A 6 5
              ♥ K 7
              ♦ A 6 2
              ♣ A 10 6 5 3
```

West	North	East	South
–	–	–	1NT (15–17)
Pass	3NT	End	

West leads the ♠J against 3NT. How will you play the contract?

You have seven tricks on top and must develop the club suit to provide two more tricks. Suppose you win the spade lead and play ace, king and another club. That's no good! East will win the third round of clubs and may well switch to the ♥Q. You will then lose four heart tricks, going one down.

East is the danger hand because he can lead through your ♥K.

You must therefore aim to set up the club suit without allowing East on lead. Win the spade lead with the king, cash the ♣K and lead the ♣2 to your ♣10. You are 'ducking into the safe hand'. West wins with the ♣J and cannot attack hearts profitably from his side of the table. You will win his return and score nine tricks: four club tricks and five top winners in the other suits.

How to play a stopper of A-J-x

When you hold A-J-x in the suit that has been led against no-trumps, you can think of your holding as one-and-a-half stoppers. The ace is a certain stopper and the J-x may provide a second stopper. When a low card is led and your right-hand opponent plays the king or the queen, you may need to think carefully whether to take your ace on the first round. The decision will usually depend on which defender is expected to gain the lead. Look at this deal:

```
                    ♠ 7 3
                    ♥ A Q 9
                    ♦ K 6 3 2
                    ♣ Q J 10 4
    ♠ Q 10 8 6 4       ┌─────────┐        ♠ K 9 5
    ♥ 10 5 3           │    N    │        ♥ J 8 7 4
    ♦ 10 7          │ W     E │        ♦ Q J 9 4
    ♣ K 6 5           │    S    │        ♣ 8 2
                    └─────────┘
                    ♠ A J 2
                    ♥ K 6 2
                    ♦ A 8 5
                    ♣ A 9 7 3
```

West	North	East	South
–	–	–	1NT (15–17)
Pass	3NT	End	

West leads the ♠6 against 3NT and East plays the ♠K. How will you play the contract?

Before deciding whether to win with the ♠A, you must make a plan for the whole deal. You have seven top tricks and will therefore need to establish two extra tricks from somewhere. The obvious source of these tricks is in clubs, where you can take a finesse through East. If the finesse wins, there will be no problem; you will have four club tricks, more than enough for the contract. What if the finesse loses? West will then be on lead and you will need to have some protection left in spades. So, you should win with the ♠A immediately. Your remaining ♠J-2 will then act as a stopper in spades (with West on lead). You cross to dummy with the ♥Q and run the ♣Q. This loses to the ♣K but the contract is safe. With West on lead, you still have a guard in the spade suit.

Let's alter the club suit on that last deal, to show that it is not always right to win the first round when you hold an A-J-x stopper:

```
              ♠ 7 3
              ♥ A Q 9
              ♦ K 6 3 2
              ♣ A 9 7 3
♠ Q 10 8 6 4              ♠ K 9 5
♥ 10 5 3        N         ♥ J 8 7 4
♦ 10 7       W   E        ♦ Q J 9 4
♣ 8 6 5         S         ♣ K 2
              ♠ A J 2
              ♥ K 6 2
              ♦ A 8 5
              ♣ Q J 10 4
```

West	North	East	South
–	–	–	1NT (15–17)
Pass	3NT	End	

West again leads the ♠6 to East's ♠K. As before, you will need to develop the club suit to bring your total to nine tricks. The difference here is that it is East who will gain the lead if the club finesse fails. As you see, you will go down if you win the first round of spades. When East wins with the ♣K he will return the ♠9 through your ♠J-2 and the defenders will claim four spade tricks to put you one down.

You must adopt a different approach – holding up the ♠A until the third round so that you can exhaust East's spades. You allow the ♠K to win. When he returns the ♠9, you insert the ♠J and West wins with the ♠Q. West is welcome to clear the spade suit because when you subsequently take a club finesse East will have no spade to return. (If he did hold another spade, the suit would have broken 4–4 and provide no threat to the contract.)

So, with a stopper of A-J-x you must plan the whole contract, seeing which defender is likely to gain the lead. If it is your left-hand opponent, you will win the first trick. If it is your right-hand opponent, you will hold up the ace until the third round.

Alter your normal play in a suit

Sometimes the normal best play in a suit is to take a finesse. When this would be into the danger hand, it may be prudent to follow a different line, thereby improving your chance of making the contract. Look at the diamond suit on this 3NT contract:

```
              ♠ 7 3
              ♥ A K 9
              ♦ K J 6 3
              ♣ A K 5 3

♠ 10 6 5                        ♠ K Q J 9 4
♥ J 8 7 3        N              ♥ 10 5 4
♦ 10 9 7      W     E           ♦ Q 8
♣ J 9 6          S              ♣ Q 10 8

              ♠ A 8 2
              ♥ Q 6 2
              ♦ A 5 4 2
              ♣ 7 4 2
```

West	North	East	South
–	1♣	1♠	1NT
Pass	3NT	End	

West leads the ♣5 against 3NT. How will you play the contract?

You should hold up the ♠A until the third round, to exhaust West's cards in the suit. What then? You have eight top tricks and must develop a ninth trick in one of the minor suits. As we saw on an earlier deal, the odds of doing this in clubs are not good; even if the suit does break 3–3 there is a big risk that East will gain the lead and be able to cash two more spade winners. So, look for your ninth trick in diamonds. What is the best play in that suit?

If you needed four diamond tricks for the contract, you would finesse the ♦J, hoping to find West with ♦Q-x-x (or ♦Q-x). Here you need only three diamond tricks for the contract. You should therefore begin with the king and ace of the suit. If the ♦Q does not fall, little has been lost. You can still lead towards dummy's ♦J on the third round, making the contract when West held the ♦Q all along. All you will have lost is an overtrick. The (huge) benefit comes when East begins with a doubleton ♦Q. The card will fall and you will make the contract where an early finesse would have led to defeat.

Sometimes the normal play in a suit is to play for the drop – when you are missing four cards to the queen, for example. When such a play would risk the danger hand gaining the lead, it may be prudent to take a finesse instead. That's the case on this deal:

```
                    ♠ 7 3
                    ♥ A 9 6 4
                    ♦ A 4 3 2
                    ♣ K 8 4
  ♠ A J 9 6 5                         ♠ 10 8 4
  ♥ Q 8 3          ┌─────────┐        ♥ J 10 7 5
  ♦ 6              │   N     │        ♦ Q 10 8
  ♣ Q 10 7 2      │ W   E   │        ♣ J 6 5
                   │   S     │
                   └─────────┘
                    ♠ K Q 2
                    ♥ K 2
                    ♦ K J 9 7 5
                    ♣ A 9 3
```

West	North	East	South
–	*–*	*–*	1NT (15–17)
Pass	2♣	Pass	2♦
Pass	3NT	End	

West leads the ♣6 against 3NT and East plays the ♣10. How will you tackle the contract?

You win the first trick with the ♣Q and see that you have seven top tricks. The diamond suit should provide the two extra tricks that are needed, but it must be developed without allowing East (the danger hand, who can lead through your remaining ♠K-2) to gain the lead.

Suppose you make the 'normal' play in diamonds, cashing the ace and king. You will no longer be able to make the contract! East will gain the lead on the next round of diamonds and a spade return will be fatal. So, you should cross to the ♦A and then finesse the ♦J. As it happens, the finesse will win and you will end with an overtrick. That is not the purpose of the play, however. Even if the finesse had lost to a doubleton ♦Q with West, the contract would be secure. You would still have the four diamond tricks that you need and the safe hand would be on lead, unable to continue spades effectively.

Lead through a defender's high card

Many a contract can be made by the simple technique of leading a low card through a defender's high card towards an honour in the third hand. If the defender plays his high card on thin air he will promote your remaining honours and give you an extra trick. If, instead, he plays low, you can pocket one trick and perhaps turn your attention elsewhere while your protection in the enemy suit remains intact.

It's not easy to visualize, so let's look at a typical deal featuring this technique:

```
                    ♠ 7 2
                    ♥ K 8 5
                    ♦ Q J 5 4
                    ♣ A Q 6 4
   ♠ 8 5                            ♠ K J 10 9 6
   ♥ 9 7 3 2         N              ♥ A 10 4
   ♦ 10 8 7 3     W     E           ♦ A 9 6
   ♣ 9 7 2           S              ♣ 10 3
                    ♠ A Q 4 3
                    ♥ Q J 6
                    ♦ K 2
                    ♣ K J 8 5
```

West	North	East	South
–	–	1♠	1NT
Pass	3NT	End	

West leads the ♠8 against 3NT. East overtakes with the ♠9 and you win with the ♠Q. How will you play the contract?

You have six top tricks in the black suits and therefore need to score three tricks from the red suits. No red suit on its own is likely to provide three easy tricks. Suppose you lead the ♦K at Trick 2. That's no good. East will win with the ♦A and clear the spade suit. You will score only two red-suit tricks (in diamonds) and East will be able to beat the contract the moment you play on hearts. Your fate will be the same if you play a heart at Trick 2. East will win and clear the spades, again restricting you to eight tricks.

The winning play is to cross to dummy with a club at Trick 2 and to lead a low diamond through East's ♦A towards your ♦K. Do you see the point of this? If East rises with the ♦A on thin air, you will have three diamond tricks, enough for the contract. If, instead, East plays low, as he probably will do, you will score one diamond trick (with the ♦K) without having to release your last spade stopper in exchange. You can then switch to hearts, setting up the second and third red-suit tricks that you need.

The next deal is on the same theme. You lead a low card through the defender's high card. Whether or not he rises with it, you will make the contract.

```
                    ♠ A K Q J
                    ♥ K J 4 2
                    ♦ 8 5
                    ♣ Q 8 7
   ♠ 10 8 7 6 3        N         ♠ 5 2
   ♥ A            W       E      ♥ 9 8 5
   ♦ A Q 6 3          S         ♦ J 10 9 2
   ♣ A 10 5                      ♣ J 9 6 4
                    ♠ 9 4
                    ♥ Q 10 7 6 3
                    ♦ K 7 4
                    ♣ K 3 2
```

West	North	East	South
1♠	1NT	Pass	3♥
Pass	4♥	End	

West leads the ♠6 against your game in hearts. How will you play the contract?

Suppose you win the spade lead, draw trumps and immediately take some discards on the spades. You will go down whichever minor-suit cards you decide to throw. Suppose you throw the ♣3-2. When you play the ♣K to West's ♣A, you will set up the ♣Q as a winner. It will not be much use, though, because you can only throw one diamond from your hand and will still lose two diamond tricks to go down.

To make the contract you must lead a club from the South hand, through West's ace, before deciding what to throw on dummy's spade winners. If West rises with the ace, you will have two club tricks and make the contract easily. If, instead, he plays low, you will discard both your remaining clubs on the spades and not lose a single club trick.

How does the play go? At Trick 2 you lead the king of trumps to West's ace. You win the spade continuation, cross to the queen of trumps and draw East's last trump with the ten. You then lead a low club through West's ace. He will doubtless play low, unwilling to give you two club tricks. You win with dummy's ♣Q and play two more spade winners, throwing your last two clubs. You can then afford to lose two diamond tricks, eventually ruffing the third round of diamonds in dummy to make the game.

So, remember that you can often steal a trick by leading towards an honour, through a high card held by a defender. You may then be able to make the contract whether or not he decides to rise with his high card in the second seat.

Points to remember

- It often happens that one defender is a 'safe hand', the other is a 'danger hand'. When you have a choice of two finesses to take, you should generally prefer the one that is into the safe hand.

- Similarly, when you are seeking to establish a suit you should try to duck a trick into the safe hand rather than into the danger hand.

- When you have a two-way finesse to take, and can afford to lose a trick in order to set up an extra trick, finesse into the safe hand.

- The best play in a suit may be affected by the fact that one of the defenders is a 'danger hand'. For example, you may try to drop the missing honour in the danger hand before eventually playing for the safe hand to hold that card.

- You can sometimes steal a trick by leading through a defender's high card towards an honour that you hold.

Test yourself

(1)

```
            ♠ K 5 2
            ♥ A 6 4
            ♦ A Q J 4
            ♣ 8 5 4
♥J led
                    N
                W       E
                    S

            ♠ A J 10 9 7 3
            ♥ 2
            ♦ K 9 7
            ♣ K 7 3
```

West	North	East	South
–	1♦	Pass	1♠
Pass	1NT	Pass	4♠
End			

West leads the ♥J against your spade game. How will you play the contract?

(2)

```
            ♠ 2
            ♥ A 8 6 4
            ♦ A J 5 4
            ♣ A 9 5 4
♠6 led
                    N
                W       E
                    S

            ♠ A J 7
            ♥ K 2
            ♦ K 10 8 7 3
            ♣ K 7 3
```

West	North	East	South
–	–	–	1♦
Pass	1♥	Pass	1NT
Pass	3NT	End	

How will you play 3NT when West leads the ♠6 and East plays the ♠Q?

Answers

(1)

```
                          ♠ K 5 2
                          ♥ A 6 4
                          ♦ A Q J 4
                          ♣ 8 5 4
        ♠ 6                                  ♠ Q 8 4
        ♥ J 10 9 3          N               ♥ K Q 8 7 5
        ♦ 10 6 5 3      W       E           ♦ 8 2
        ♣ A Q 9 2          S               ♣ J 10 6
                          ♠ A J 10 9 7 3
                          ♥ 2
                          ♦ K 9 7
                          ♣ K 7 3
```

West	North	East	South
–	1♦	Pass	1♠
Pass	1NT	Pass	4♠
End			

West leads the ♥J against your spade game. You win and play the ♠K. If you continue with spade to the ace, West showing out, you will go down. When you switch to diamonds, hoping to discard one of your club losers in time, East will ruff the third round. He will then switch to the ♣J, giving the defenders three tricks in that suit.

To keep the dangerous East hand off lead, you should finesse the ♠J on the second round. As it happens, the finesse will win. You will not lose a trump trick and can discard one of your clubs on the fourth round of diamonds, ending with an overtrick.

The point of this play is that you will make the contract whether or not the trump finesse wins. Suppose West wins the second round of trumps from an original holding of ♠Q-6. He cannot attack clubs effectively from his side of the table. He will probably play another heart. You will ruff and play four rounds of diamonds, discarding one of your club losers on the fourth round. The spade finesse on the second round is a win–win play that guarantees the contract.

(2)

```
              ♠ 2
              ♥ A 8 6 4
              ♦ A J 5 4
              ♣ A 9 5 4
♠ K 10 8 6 3      N        ♠ Q 9 5 4
♥ J 10 9 3    W     E      ♥ Q 7 5
♦ 6               S        ♦ Q 9 2
♣ Q 10 2                   ♣ J 8 6
              ♠ A J 7
              ♥ K 2
              ♦ K 10 8 7 3
              ♣ K 7 3
```

West	North	East	South
–	–	–	1♦
Pass	1♥	Pass	1NT
Pass	3NT	End	

How will you play 3NT when West leads the ♠6 and East plays the ♠Q?

You should win with the ♠A, retaining the ♠J-7 as a partial stopper in the suit. You now need to develop nine tricks without allowing East (the danger hand, who can lead through your spade tenace) on lead. You have seven tricks on top and can easily develop two more from the diamond suit, even if you take a losing finesse there. You should cross to the ♦A and then finesse the ♦10.

When the cards lie as in the diagram, the finesse will win. Suppose it had lost to a doubleton queen with West, though. You would still make 3NT. You would have four diamond tricks, enough for the contract, and the safe hand would be on lead. West cannot profitably continue spades from his side of the table.

05

weak two-bids

In this chapter you will learn:
- when to open with a weak two-bid
- how to respond to a weak two-bid
- the 2NT relay response
- how to bid a strong two-bid hand.

What does an opening bid of 2♦, 2♥ or 2♠ mean? In the early days of bridge such an opening showed a strong hand, in some parts of the world a very strong hand! Indeed, strong two-bids are still in general use when playing rubber bridge. They were described in the companion volume, *Teach Yourself Bridge*.

One of the defects of strong two-bids is that they rarely arise. You are not often dealt a hand so powerful that you fear a missed game if you open with a one-bid. In any case, when you hold a really big hand you can open 2♣. So, it is almost universal in tournament bridge to use the opening bids of 2♦, 2♥ and 2♠ to show a weak hand. The hand will be similar in nature to a weak 3♦, 3♥ or 3♠ opening but it will contain a six-card suit rather than a seven-card suit.

Open 2♦ when you hold 6–10 points and six diamonds.
Open 2♥ when you hold 6–10 points and six hearts.
Open 2♠ when you hold 6–10 points and six spades.

The ideal hand for a weak two-bid will contain a respectable six-card suit. These are all worthy specimens:

a	b	c
♠ 6 3	♠ K Q J 8 6 2	♠ 10 6
♥ 10 9 4	♥ 8 3	♥ K J 10 8 4 2
♦ A Q 10 8 7 4	♦ K J 2	♦ 7
♣ 7 2	♣ 10 2	♣ J 9 5 2

Hand **a** represents a minimum weak 2♦ opening. It is still an ideal weak two-bid because the suit is so strong. Hand **b** is a maximum weak 2♠ bid. Hand **c** contains only five points but the suit is strong and, when non-vulnerable, you would stretch to open with a weak 2♥ bid.

Let's look now at three less respectable specimens, ones that contain a defect of some sort. Whether you are willing to open a weak two-bid on such hands depends on your style. If you like to cause the maximum amount of disruption to the opponents' bidding and are willing to accept an increased risk of a bad result of your own, go ahead and open!

a	b	c
♠ 6 3	♠ J 9 8 6 5 2	♠ K Q J 8 3
♥ J 9 8 4	♥ A 3	♥ 8 7 5
♦ K Q 10 9 6 4	♦ 9 4	♦ J 7
♣ J	♣ K Q 5	♣ Q 10 4

Hand **a** contains a four-card major on the side. Many players are unwilling to open a weak-two on such a hand, fearing that they will miss a fit in the major suit. Bear in mind, though, that if you do hold a good heart fit the opponents are likely to hold a big spade fit and may outbid you anyway. Hand **b** is not particularly suitable because only 1 of the 10 points is in the long suit. You have much more defence to an opponent's contract than partner will imagine. Hand **c** contains only a five-card suit. Nevertheless, many tournament players would open 2♠. By doing so, they would suggest a good opening lead to partner and make life difficult for the opponents.

You get the idea, then. There is the 'classical weak-two', with everything in order and all the boxes ticked. There is also the 'undisciplined weak-two', which may contain one or more flaws. It is up to you which style you prefer to adopt.

Responding to a weak two-bid

When your partner opens with a weak two-bid, you will have a fairly accurate picture of his hand and can often place the contract immediately. Remember that the opening may be based on quite a weak hand. If you have 12 or 13 points and no particular fit, it will often be right to pass. Against that, when you have a good trump fit, it may be a good move to feign strength and raise partner. You hope to make life even more difficult for the player on your left.

These are the possible responses to an opening 2♥ bid:

2♠ / 3♣ / 3♦	Natural and forcing
2NT	A relay bid to ask for more information
3♥	Pre-emptive – partner must pass
3NT / 4♠	To play
4♥	May be strong; may be pre-emptive

The responses to 2♦ and 2♠ are along the same lines. We will look at the 2NT relay bid, asking for more information, in a moment. Meanwhile, what response would you make on the hands below?

West	North	East	South
2♥	Pass	?	

a ♠ A K 4	**b** ♠ K Q 9	**c** ♠ K 9 7 2
♥ 6	♥ A 3	♥ 4 2
♦ Q 10 8	♦ A K J 2	♦ K J 8 2
♣ A K Q 10 7 2	♣ 10 8 7 2	♣ A J 6

On **a** you can see that 3NT is likely to be a better game than either 4♥ or 5♣. So, respond with a simple 3NT. On **b** you have a 6–2 fit in hearts and can expect there to be good play for a heart game. Respond 4♥. With hand **c** game prospects are poor. Even if partner holds ♥A-K-Q-x-x-x, you are still some way from game. You should therefore pass.

The 2NT relay bid

Since a single raise of partner's suit is pre-emptive (2♥ – 3♥, for example), you cannot follow such a route when you wish to make a game try in partner's suit. In such a situation you respond 2NT, a relay bid that asks partner to give you a further definition of his hand. These are the rebids by the opener after a start of 2♦ – 2NT, 2♥ – 2NT or 2♠ – 2NT:

3♣	Lower-range, suit has 1 (or 0) top honours (A-K-Q)
3♦	Lower-range, suit has 2 top honours
3♥	Upper-range, suit has 1 (or 0) top honours
3♠	Upper-range, suit has 2 top honours
3NT	Suit is headed by the A-K-Q

So, when you are uncertain whether or not to bid game, you respond 2NT. When partner shows an upper-range opening, you can bid game. This is a typical sequence:

West	North	East	South
♠ K Q 9 8 5 3	♠ A 10 4	2♠	2NT
♥ Q 8	♥ K J 6 3	3♠	4♠
♦ Q 10 6	♦ 9 8		
♣ 9 3	♣ A Q J 5		

East holds 15 points and does not expect game to be a good bet opposite a lower-range opening. He responds with the 2NT relay and hears that West is upper-range with two of the three top trump honours. He bids 4♠ and this proves to be a worthwhile prospect.

Bidding is not an exact science. With the East hand we have just seen, game would be a good prospect opposite some lower-range hands; it would be a poor prospect opposite some upper-range hands. Still, you can tilt the odds in your favour by discovering more about the opener's hand.

What if I hold a strong two-bid?

If you normally play strong two-bids, you are no doubt wondering how to cope with such hands when you start to play weak two-bids. The answer is that you must either open with a one-bid, trusting that it will not be passed out, or you must open with a full-blooded 2♣. As a general guideline, lean towards a 2♣ opening when you have a very high point-count. When, instead, you hold a moderate point-count and massive playing strength, it is usually safe to open with a one-bid.

Playing weak two-bids, what opening would you choose on these hands?

a ♠ A K Q 9 7 2   b ♠ K 2   c ♠ A K 9
  ♥ Q J 10 8 7 6   ♥ 3   ♥ A K Q 9 8 6
  ♦ 8   ♦ A K Q J 9 2   ♦ 2
  ♣ –   ♣ A Q J 8   ♣ K Q 6

On hand **a** you want to end in game, yes, but you cannot open 2♣ on a hand with so few high cards and so little defence. Open 1♠ and it will very rarely be passed out. Your intention, given the chance, is to rebid 4♥ to offer partner a choice of games. On **b** you can open 1♦. Someone or other will surely find a bid in one of the majors.

On **c** you will open 2♣. If you open 1♥ you not only risk this being passed out when you have a cold game, you will also find it difficult to bid a slam when partner has modest values and length in one of the black suits.

Points to remember

- A classical weak two-bid contains 6–10 points and a six-card suit headed by at least one of the three top honours. No four-card major will be held on the side.

- Some players are happy to open a weak-two when the hand contains one or more flaws. There may be a four-card major on the side, for example; the long major may be weak or contain only five cards; or the high-card strength may be below 6–10 points.

- A single raise of a weak-two (2♥ – 3♥) is pre-emptive and the opener should not bid again. A game raise (2♥ – 4♥) may be on a strong hand, where you expect to make the contract, or on a weaker hand with four-card trump support. In the latter case, you hope to shut the opponents out from a good contract their way.

- A response in a new suit is forcing. Responder may also use a relay bid of 2NT. The opener will then reply on a five-step basis, the first two steps showing a lower-range hand with and without two top honours. The next two steps show an upper-range hand with and without two of the three top honours. The fifth step shows A-K-Q in the trump suit.

Test yourself

(1) Playing weak two-bids, what opening bid (if any) would you make on the following hands?

a	♠ 9	b	♠ A Q 8 2	c	♠ A 8 6
	♥ 10 2		♥ K J 10 7 6 4		♥ J 7 6 5 3 2
	♦ Q J 10 8 3 2		♦ 9 3		♦ 8 2
	♣ K 9 8 4		♣ 4		♣ A 10

(2) What will you respond on the following East hands when your partner opens with a weak two-bid in hearts?

West	North	East	South
2♥	Pass	?	

a	♠ 5 3	b	♠ A Q 9 6 4	c	♠ A Q 8
	♥ A 8 4 2		♥ 3		♥ 9 3
	♦ Q J 10 8 4 2		♦ A K Q 6		♦ A 9 7 2
	♣ 4		♣ Q 7 3		♣ Q J 8 2

(3) What will you rebid on the following West hands when your partner has responded with a 2NT relay bid?

West	North	East	South
2♠	Pass	2NT	Pass
?			

a ♠ A Q 9 7 6 2   b ♠ K Q 10 8 7 4   c ♠ Q J 10 8 7 2
♥ 10 2   ♥ 9 8 6   ♥ J 3
♦ J 10 7   ♦ 6   ♦ A J 6 4
♣ 9 3   ♣ K J 6   ♣ 5

Answers

(1) a **2♠**. Perfect for a weak two-bid. You have some solidity in the long suit and the four-card clubs will assist the playing strength.

  b **1♠**. You should not open a weak 2♥ when you have such a strong four-card spade suit on the side. A pass is possible, but the hand is worth a one-bid.

  c **Pass**. In general, a pre-emptive bid should have good playing strength if trumps are chosen and little defence if the opponents choose trumps. Here the opposite is the case. The heart suit is very weak and there are two aces on the side. If you open such hands with a pre-empt, it is difficult for partner to judge what to do later in the bidding.

(2) a **4♥**. With four-card support and a reasonable six-card side suit, you do not expect to lose a big penalty in 4♥. At the same time there is every reason to expect that the opponents can make a big contract in one of the black suits. Make life difficult for them with a pre-emptive raise!

  b **2♠**. There may well be a game available somewhere. Begin with a forcing bid in a new suit, hoping that partner can raise.

  c **Pass**. It is very unlikely that you can make game. Certainly you would not be justified in responding 2NT and advancing to game just because partner told you he was upper-range.

(3) a **3♦**. Lower-range with two top honours.

  b **3♠**. Upper-range with two top honours.

  c **3♥**. Upper-range without two top honours.

playing a dummy reversal

In this chapter you will learn:
- how to play a dummy reversal
- how to score the low trumps in the long-trump hand.

One of the advantages of playing in a suit contract, rather than in no-trumps, is that you can score extra tricks by ruffing. To do this, you normally have to ruff in the short-trump hand. Suppose this is your trump suit:

North
♠ J 7 4

South
♠ A K Q 10 3

You begin with five trump tricks. If you take one ruff in the hand with three trumps, you will score a total of six trump tricks: five in the South hand and one extra for the ruff in dummy. Suppose instead that you ruff something in the long-trump (South) hand. It will not give you an extra trick. It will merely consume one of the trump tricks that you could have scored anyway. So, although there may be some technical reason to ruff in the long-trump hand (for example, you may be trying to set up a side suit in dummy), it will not give you an extra trick directly.

To make sure this is clear, here is a deal that incorporates the trump suit above:

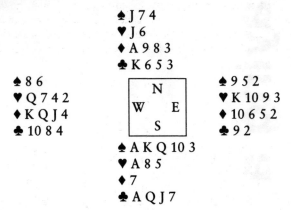

Imagine that you are in 6♠ and West leads the ♦K. How would you play the contract?

You can count eleven top tricks: five rounds of trumps, two red aces and four club tricks. To score a twelfth trick, you must ruff a heart in the short-trump hand (North). So, win the diamond lead and play ace and another heart. You ruff the diamond return, ruff a heart with the ♠J and then draw trumps. You have made six trump tricks and six tricks in the side suits. The slam is yours.

Suppose, instead, you were to ruff one or two diamonds in the long-trump (South) hand. It would not help you at all! You would still make only five trump tricks and leave your total at eleven tricks.

With this important preamble out of the way, we will look at a style of play where you break the normal rule by taking ruffs in the long-trump hand. As we will see, if you can take enough ruffs in the long-trump hand you can actually create an extra trick.

What is a dummy reversal?

If you can take so many ruffs in the long-trump hand that it ends up becoming the short-trump hand, you will score an extra trump trick. Look at this trump suit:

> *North*
>
> ♠ Q J 4
>
> *South*
>
> ♠ A K 10 3 2

If you can take as many as three ruffs in the South hand, you will score a total of six trump tricks. You will score three ruffs with the 2, 10 and king, then three trump tricks with the ace, queen and jack. Here is a complete deal where this style of play is necessary.

	♠ Q J 4	
	♥ J 7 6	
	♦ K Q 2	
	♣ A 7 5 2	
♠ 9 6		♠ 8 7 5
♥ A Q 4	N	♥ K 9 8 3
♦ J 9 8 3	W　E	♦ 10 5
♣ Q J 10 3	S	♣ K 9 8 4
	♠ A K 10 3 2	
	♥ 10 5 2	
	♦ A 7 6 4	
	♣ 6	

West	North	East	South
–	1♣	Pass	1♠
Pass	1NT (12–14)	Pass	2♦
Pass	2♠	Pass	4♠
End			

West leads the ♣Q against your game in spades. How will you play the contract?

Suppose first that you look at the losers from the South seat. You have three top losers in hearts and a potential further loser on the fourth round of diamonds. How can you avoid a diamond loser? The main chance is that the diamonds will break 3–3. Another possibility is to draw just two rounds of trumps and continue with the three top diamonds. Playing this way, you would also make the contract when diamonds broke 4–2 but the defender with the doubleton diamond did not hold the last trump. (You would be able to ruff your fourth diamond in the dummy.) Neither of these chances would come home, as the cards lie, and the contract would go down if you played that way.

Now look at the losers from the North viewpoint. You still have the three heart losers. If you can ruff the three further potential losers in the club suit, you will make the contract! How should the play go? After winning the club lead, you should ruff a club immediately with the ♠2. You then play the ace and queen of trumps. When trumps break 3–2, you know it is right to continue with the dummy reversal. You ruff another club with the ♠10, return to dummy with the ♦K and ruff dummy's last club with the ♠K. Finally, you return to dummy with the ♦Q, draw the outstanding trump and score the ♦A for your tenth trick. You scored six trump tricks and four side-suit winners.

What if two rounds of trumps had revealed a 4–1 break? It would no longer be possible to play a dummy reversal, since you would not be able to draw trumps after taking three ruffs. You would continue instead with the three top diamonds, hoping that diamonds were 3–3, or the defender with four trumps also held four diamonds.

Scoring the low trumps

Another reason to take ruffs in the long-trump hand is to score the low trumps there. Suppose this is your trump holding:

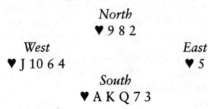

North
♥ 9 8 2

West   *East*
♥ J 10 6 4   ♥ 5

South
♥ A K Q 7 3

You cannot score five trump tricks simply by drawing trumps, since the defenders' trumps are breaking 4–1. What you need to do is to score the ♥7 and ♥3 by taking ruffs in the long-trump hand. That is the winning line of play on this deal:

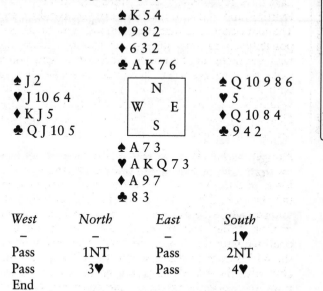

♠ K 5 4
♥ 9 8 2
♦ 6 3 2
♣ A K 7 6

♠ J 2
♥ J 10 6 4
♦ K J 5
♣ Q J 10 5

♠ Q 10 9 8 6
♥ 5
♦ Q 10 8 4
♣ 9 4 2

♠ A 7 3
♥ A K Q 7 3
♦ A 9 7
♣ 8 3

West	North	East	South
–	–	–	1♥
Pass	1NT	Pass	2NT
Pass	3♥	Pass	4♥
End			

West leads the ♣Q and you win with dummy's ♣A. When you play two rounds of trumps, East discards a spade on the second round. You now seem to have three side-suit losers (one in spades, two in diamonds) in addition to a certain trump loser. What can you do about it?

On this particular deal you must look at your winners instead of your losers. You have five winners in the side suits. If you can score all five trumps in your hand, this will bring the total to ten. In other words, you must aim to ruff two clubs in the South hand. How does the play go?

You draw a third round of trumps with the queen, return to dummy with the ♣K and ruff a club with the ♥3. You return to dummy with the ♠K and lead the last club. East shows out and you ruff with the ♥7, West having to follow suit. You score the two aces still in your hand, bringing the total to ten tricks.

You may wonder what happened to the defenders' four 'certain' tricks. The answer is that West will have to ruff his partner's spade winner at the end!

Points to remember

- Generally speaking, a ruff in the short-trump hand will give you an extra trick. A ruff in the long-trump hand will not produce an extra trick.
- If you take several ruffs in the long-trump hand (so that it ends with fewer trumps than the hand opposite), you can create an extra trick. Playing in this way is known as 'reversing the dummy'.
- A dummy reversal may be possible only when the trumps break favourably (because you will eventually have to draw trumps in the short-trump hand). In such a situation you should aim to test the trump suit before embarking on the dummy reversal.
- It may be beneficial to ruff in the long-trump hand simply with the aim of scoring the low trumps there.

Test yourself

(1)

♠ 8 5 3
♥ A 6 3
♦ A K 7
♣ 10 8 5 4

♦Q led

```
        N
    W       E
        S
```

♠ A K Q 6 2
♥ K 7
♦ 8 3
♣ A 7 6 3

West	North	East	South
–	–	–	1♠
Pass	2♣	Pass	4♣
Pass	4♠	End	

West leads the ♦Q. You win with the ♦A and draw two rounds of trumps, East throwing a diamond on the second round. How will you continue?

(2)

♠ K J 9
♥ 8 6 3
♦ A 5 2
♣ A 8 5 2

♣Q led

```
      N
  W       E
      S
```

♠ A Q 10 6 3
♥ A K Q 2
♦ K 9 6
♣ 7

West	North	East	South
–	1♣	Pass	1♠
Pass	1NT	Pass	3♥
Pass	3♠	Pass	4NT
Pass	5♣	Pass	6♠
End			

West leads the ♣Q against your small slam in spades. How will you play the contract?

Answers

(1)

```
              ♠ 8 5 3
              ♥ A 6 3
              ♦ A K 7
              ♣ 10 8 5 4
♠ J 10 9 4                      ♠ 7
♥ Q 10 8 2      ┌─────────┐     ♥ J 9 5 4
♦ Q J 10 5      │    N    │     ♦ 9 6 4 2
♣ 2             │  W   E  │     ♣ K Q J 9
                │    S    │
                └─────────┘
              ♠ A K Q 6 2
              ♥ K 7
              ♦ 8 3
              ♣ A 7 6 3
```

West	North	East	South
–	–	–	1♠
Pass	2♣	Pass	4♣
Pass	4♠	End	

West leads the ♦Q against your spade game. You win with the ♦A in dummy and draw two rounds of trumps, East discarding a diamond on the second round. How will you continue?

If clubs break 3–2, you can simply draw one more round of trumps and play ace and another club. You win the diamond return and set up a long card in clubs, still with control of the trump suit. You must next ask yourself whether there is a line of play that will succeed when the clubs break 4–1.

The best line of play is (how did you guess?) a dummy reversal. You have five winners in the side suits. If you can score all five trumps in the South hand, the total will come to ten whether or not the clubs break 3–2. You draw a third round of trumps, cash the ♣A and cross to the ♦K to ruff a diamond in your hand. You continue with king, ace and another heart, ruffing once again in the South hand. The contract is yours and, with the clubs 4–1, you could not have made the contract any other way.

(2)

```
                        ♠ K J 9
                        ♥ 8 6 3
                        ♦ A 5 2
                        ♣ A 8 5 2
    ♠ 8 7 5                              ♠ 4 2
    ♥ 7 4           ┌─────────┐         ♥ J 10 9 5
    ♦ Q 10 8        │    N    │         ♦ J 7 4 3
    ♣ Q J 10 9 4    │  W   E  │         ♣ K 6 3
                    │    S    │
                    └─────────┘
                        ♠ A Q 10 6 3
                        ♥ A K Q 2
                        ♦ K 9 6
                        ♣ 7
```

West	North	East	South
–	1♣	Pass	1♠
Pass	1NT	Pass	3♥
Pass	3♠	Pass	4NT
Pass	5♣	Pass	6♠
End			

West leads the ♣Q against your small slam in spades. How will you play the contract?

You have six winners in the side suits. If you can score three club ruffs in the South hand, playing a dummy reversal, you will be able to add six trump tricks to your total.

You win the club lead in dummy and ruff a club with the ♠10. You return to dummy with the ♦A and ruff another club with the ♠Q. A trump to the nine allows you to ruff dummy's last club with the ♠A. You then lead your last trump to dummy's king and draw the last trump with the jack. Twelve tricks are yours.

07

playing a forcing defence

In this chapter you will learn:
- how to play a forcing defence
- when it is right to hold up the ace of trumps.

When you are defending, declarer will usually start with more trumps than you do. However, if you can force him to ruff enough times, in the long-trump holding, you may end up with more trumps than he does. This style of play is known as 'playing a forcing defence'. Let's see an example of it.

```
                    ♠ J 10 6
                    ♥ 9 7 6 2
                    ♦ 10 3 2
                    ♣ A Q 5
    ♠ 8 5 4 2                          ♠ 7
    ♥ A K Q 10 3        N             ♥ 8 5
    ♦ A 4          W         E        ♦ 9 8 7 5
    ♣ 10 9              S             ♣ J 8 7 6 4 2
                    ♠ A K Q 9 3
                    ♥ J 4
                    ♦ K Q J 6
                    ♣ K 3
```

West	North	East	South
–	–	–	1♠
2♥	2♠	Pass	4♠
End			

Sitting West, you launch the defence with the ace and king of hearts, everyone following. What now?

Suppose you try your luck with the ♣10. Declarer will win and draw trumps in four rounds. He will then set up the diamonds and claim an easy ten tricks. Instead, you must attack declarer's trump holding, hoping that he started with just five trumps to your four.

After cashing two top hearts, you should continue with another heart winner. Declarer ruffs and now has the same number of trumps as you. He can no longer make the contract! He will doubtless draw two rounds of trumps, discovering the 4–1 trump break. If he draws your remaining two trumps, he will have no trumps left in his own hand. When you win with the ♦A you will be able to cash two heart winners.

What will happen if declarer chooses instead to play on diamonds without drawing your trumps? You will win and play yet another heart, forcing him to ruff again. You will then have two trumps to declarer's one. He will have 'lost trump control' and will go down.

Always consider a forcing defence when you hold four trumps (or suspect that partner does). By leading your own strongest side suit, you may be able to force declarer to ruff.

Holding up the ace of trumps

A trump holding of four cards to the ace is particularly valuable when you are considering a forcing defence. One reason is that you will be able to force declarer again when you win with the ace of trumps. Sometimes, though, you must calculate carefully when you should take the trump ace. This type of hand is quite common:

```
                        ♠ A Q 6
                        ♥ J 8 5
                        ♦ K 7 4
                        ♣ A 10 5 2
  ♠ 9 5                   N              ♠ 10 8 7 4 2
  ♥ A 7 6 2                              ♥ 3
  ♦ Q J 10 8 3       W        E          ♦ A 6 2
  ♣ 8 6                   S              ♣ J 9 7 4
                        ♠ K J 3
                        ♥ K Q 10 9 4
                        ♦ 9 5
                        ♣ K Q 3
```

West	North	East	South
–	–	–	1♥
Pass	2♣	Pass	2♥
Pass	4♥	End	

Sitting West, you embark on a forcing defence by leading the ♦Q. Since declarer knows that you would not lead the queen from a holding headed by the A-Q-J, he places the ♦A with East. He plays low from dummy on the first round of diamonds and low again on the second round. (This would be the winning play if East held a doubleton ♦A.) You continue with a third round of diamonds, covered by the ♦K and ♦A, and declarer ruffs. How will you continue the defence when declarer leads the ♥K at Trick 4?

Suppose you win with the ♥A. The contract will then be made. A fourth round of diamonds will not continue the 'forcing defence' because declarer will be able to ruff in dummy (in the short-trump holding). He will then be able to draw trumps and make the remaining tricks. So, how can you do better in defence?

When you take your ♥A you want to be able to continue your attack on the trump length in declarer's hand. You can do this only if you hold up your ace of trumps until the third round, when dummy's trumps will be exhausted. So, allow declarer's king to win the first round of trumps. When he plays another trump, duck again. These cards will be left:

```
                      ♠ A Q 6
                      ♥ 8
                      ♦ –
                      ♣ A 10 5 2
       ♠ 9 5                          ♠ 10 8 7 4
       ♥ A 7          N               ♥ –
       ♦ 8 3       W     E            ♦ –
       ♣ 8 6          S               ♣ J 9 7 4
                      ♠ K J 3
                      ♥ Q 10
                      ♦ –
                      ♣ K Q 3
```

Declarer has an unhappy look on his face. If he plays the ♥Q, you will win with the ♥A and play another diamond, forcing declarer to ruff (in what was the long-trump hand) with the ♥10. Your ♥7 will be the last trump out and you will also score a diamond to put the game two down. The best that declarer can do is to abandon trumps and to play black-suit winners instead. You will score a ruff with the ♥7 and that will be one down.

So, when you are playing a forcing defence and hold four trumps to the ace, think carefully when to take the ace of trumps. Do not take it early if the dummy will then have a trump left that can be used to ruff the side suit that you are using for the forcing defence.

Points to remember

• When you hold four trumps, consider playing a forcing defence. This means you lead your strongest side suit, hoping to force declarer to ruff. If declarer can be made to ruff twice, you may end up with longer trumps than he has.

- When you hold four trumps to the ace, do not take the ace of trumps on the first or second round if this will mean that declarer can use the short-trump holding (in dummy) to avoid being forced in the long-trump holding.
- Sometimes the opponents' bidding suggests that they are in a 4–4 fit. If you hold only one trump yourself, your partner will hold four trumps and a forcing defence may be successful.

Test yourself

(1)

                      ♠ A 10 7
                      ♥ 7 6 4 3
                      ♦ K J 5
                      ♣ K 9 7

    ♠ 8 5 3 2   ┌─────────┐
    ♥ K J 8 2   │   N   │
    ♦ A 8 4   │ W   E │
    ♣ 6 4   │   S   │
                       └─────────┘

West	North	East	South
–	–	–	1♠
Pass	3♠	Pass	4♠
End			

Sitting West, you embark on a forcing defence by leading the ♥2. East wins with the ♥A and continues with the ♥10 covered by South's ♥Q and your ♥K. When you play the ♥J, declarer ruffs and plays the ace and king of trumps, partner discarding a diamond on the second round. Declarer then leads the ♦2 from his hand. How will you defend?

(2)

                      ♠ 7 4 3
                      ♥ 9 7 5
                      ♦ A J 3
                      ♣ Q 9 7 5

    ♠ A K 8 6   ┌─────────┐
    ♥ K Q J 8 2   │   N   │
    ♦ 10 9   │ W   E │
    ♣ 6 4   │   S   │
                       └─────────┘

West	North	East	South
–	–	–	1♠
2♥	2♠	3♥	4♠
End			

You lead the ♥K, winning the first trick, and South ruffs the heart continuation. When he leads the ♠Q you win with the ♠K and East discards a low club. What is your plan for the defence?

Answers

(1)

```
              ♠ A 10 7
              ♥ 7 6 4 3
              ♦ K J 5
              ♣ K 9 7
♠ 8 5 3 2                      ♠ 6
♥ K J 8 2        N             ♥ A 10 5
♦ A 8 4     W         E        ♦ 10 9 7 6 3
♣ 6 4            S             ♣ 10 8 5 2
              ♠ K Q J 9 4
              ♥ Q 9
              ♦ Q 2
              ♣ A Q J 3
```

West	North	East	South
–	–	–	1♠
Pass	3♠	Pass	4♠
End			

Sitting West, with four trumps in your hand, you embark on a forcing defence by leading the ♥2. East wins with the ♥A, you are pleased to see, and continues with the ♥10 covered by the ♥Q and your ♥K. When you play the ♥J, declarer ruffs and plays the ace and king of trumps, partner discarding a diamond on the second round. Declarer now leads the ♦2 from his hand. How will you defend?

When declarer leads towards a king-jack combination in dummy, it is often right to play a smooth low card when you hold the ace in the second seat. You hope that declarer will try the jack, losing to partner's queen, and you will score two tricks in the suit. Play low here, though, and declarer will make the contract! He will score five trump tricks: four club tricks and one diamond trick.

Your forcing defence is working well and you should persevere with it. Declarer has already been reduced to the same number of trumps that you hold. So, you should rise with the ♦A and play a fourth round of hearts, forcing South to ruff again. He will then hold only one trump in each hand, while you have two trumps. He cannot draw your trumps and when he plays on the club suit you will ruff the third round for one down.

(2)

```
              ♠ 7 4 3
              ♥ 9 7 5
              ♦ A J 3
              ♣ Q 9 7 5
♠ A K 8 6        ┌─────┐        ♠ -
♥ K Q J 8 2      │  N  │        ♥ A 10 6 3
♦ 10 9         W │     │ E      ♦ 8 7 6 4
♣ 6 4            │  S  │        ♣ J 10 8 3 2
                 └─────┘
              ♠ Q J 10 9 5 2
              ♥ 4
              ♦ K Q 5 2
              ♣ A K
```

West	North	East	South
–	–	–	1♠
2♥	2♠	3♥	4♠
End			

You lead the ♥K, winning the first trick, and continue with a second round of hearts, ruffed by declarer. When he leads the queen of trumps, you win with the king and your partner discards a low club. You force declarer with another heart and he continues with the jack of trumps. What now?

If you win with the ♠A the contract will be made. A fourth round of hearts will be ineffective because declarer can ruff with dummy's last trump (in the short-trump hand). So, hold up the ace of trumps for one round.

Declarer cannot counter this defence. If he plays another trump, you will win with the ace and force his last trump with another heart. If, instead, he starts to play his winners in the minor suits, you will score a ruff with your ♠ 8.

08
negative, responsive and competitive doubles

In this chapter you will learn:
- how to use a negative double
- how to use a responsive double
- how to use a competitive double.

In the early days of bridge, the call of 'double!' had only one meaning. It indicated that you thought the opponents' contract would go down and that you wanted to increase the stakes. It was soon realized, particularly at low levels of the auction, that there was a more useful meaning for a double. It should ask partner to choose a trump suit. This is the familiar take-out double. In all the following auctions the double is for take-out, asking partner to choose between the unbid suits:

	West	North	East	South
a	1♥	Pass	Pass	Dble
b	1♦	Pass	1♠	Dble
c	3♣	Dble		
d	1♥	Pass	2♥	Dble

You may wonder which doubles are still for penalties. A double of a weak 1NT opening is a penalty double. (A penalty double of a strong 1NT is less valuable and some players use the call with a conventional meaning.) Most doubles of a game contract are for penalties. In rubber bridge a double in the following type of auction is also for penalties:

e	1♥	2♣	Dble

Even this double, though, is no longer played for penalties by the majority of tournament players. They play a double of an overcall for take-out, usually showing the two unbid suits. Such a double is known as a 'negative double'. Let's take a look at it.

The negative double

Look at this bidding problem:

West	West	North	East	South
♠ 9 3 2	–	–	1♣	1♠
♥ A J 8 2	?			
♦ Q 9 6 2				
♣ Q 7				

Your partner opens 1♣ and the next player overcalls 1♠. What do you bid?

If a double would be for penalties, as at rubber bridge, there would be no good answer to the question. You cannot bid 1NT because you have no stopper in spades. Nor are you strong enough to carry the bidding to 2♦, which would be forcing and carry your side too high when partner was minimum.

Tournament players have solved this problem by using a double of an overcall for take-out. A double here would strongly suggest four cards in the other major (hearts) and show enough points to contest the auction at this level. The opener would choose a rebid to describe the nature of his hand. With a heart fit, for example, he would rebid 2♥ with a hand in the minimum range, 3♥ or 4♥ with a stronger hand.

You can see how useful such a meaning for the double can be. Do you lose very much by not being able to double for penalties? Not at this level, certainly! When was the last time that you held such good spades that you thought the best contract for your side was one spade doubled? It would not happen very often. In any case, there is still a way to catch the opponents, as we will see in a moment.

It is best to play that doubles of an overcall are negative (for take-out) up to the level of 3♠. Let's see a hand where you might want to use a negative double at that level:

West	West	North	East	South
♠ 9 3	–	–	1♦	3♠
♥ A J 8 2	?			
♦ Q 9 6				
♣ A Q 7 3				

Without a negative double at your disposal you would, again, be completely stuck. Here you enter the auction with a negative double and wait to hear what partner says next. He may hold four hearts with you and be able to rebid 4♥. Perhaps he has a spade stopper and can rebid 3NT. If he has neither of these, and no special distribution, he may even choose to pass your double, deciding that it will be best to take a penalty against the 3♠ contract.

What happens when your partner opens the bidding and the next player overcalls in a suit that you hold strongly? You would like to make a penalty double but ... oh dear ... you have agreed to play negative doubles with your partner. All is not lost! Suppose you hold the North cards on this typical deal:

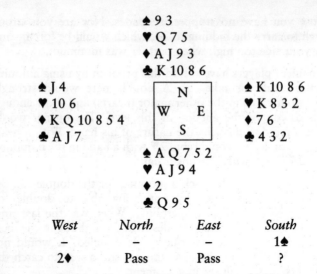

West	North	East	South
–	–	–	1♠
2♦	Pass	Pass	?

West overcalls 2♦ and, sitting North, you would like to make a penalty double. Since you are playing negative doubles, this is not possible. In such a situation, when you have a stack of trumps sitting over the overcaller, you should pass instead. If the next player passes, your partner will be able to picture the situation. He is short in diamonds himself and East did not raise the overcall. The odds are high indeed that you are sitting with a good diamond holding but could not make a penalty double. South should therefore double himself. Such a double is for take-out but is made in the hope (expectation) that partner will pass for penalties.

As you see, then, you are not paying a high price to use negative doubles. On a large proportion of the hands where you would have liked to be playing a double for penalties, your partner will re-open the bidding with a take-out double, which you will be able to pass.

The responsive double

Let's look next at yet another type of double, one that is in common usage even in rubber bridge. It is known as a 'responsive double' and arises when your partner has made a take-out double and responder raises the opener's suit before you have had a chance to reply to partner's double. This is a typical situation:

West	West	North	East	South
♠ 10 3 2	–	1♥	Dble	2♥
♥ 8 4	?			
♦ K Q 9 6				
♣ A J 7 2				

What should you bid now? With ten points you are worth a response. Suppose you respond 3♣, though. You may find that partner holds only three clubs and you had a 4–4 diamond fit. It's the same if you guess to respond 3♦. You may find that you had a better fit in clubs.

The answer is for you to make a further double yourself. Since this is in response to partner's take-out double, the call is known as a 'responsive double'. It is for take-out and asks partner to choose a trump suit. On this particular auction, partner's original double strongly suggests that he holds four spades (because spades is the 'other major'). If you held four spades yourself, you could be fairly sure that you and your partner held a 4–4 fit there. You would therefore respond 2♠ (or perhaps 3♠ or 4♠, with a stronger hand). It follows that when you make a responsive double instead you are likely to hold the two minor suits.

Again it makes good sense to play responsive doubles up to and including the level of 3♠. Here is a hand when you might make such a high-level responsive double:

West	West	North	East	South
♠ J 3	–	1♠	Dble	3♠
♥ 7 4	?			
♦ A Q 10 6 2				
♣ A 10 8 4				

Once again your best move is to double – a responsive double. With four cards in hearts you would bid 4♥ instead, expecting there to be a 4–4 fit in the suit. Your double therefore suggests length in the minor suits. You hope that partner has a spade stopper and will be able to bid 3NT. The higher the bidding is, of course, the greater the strength you will need in order to compete with a negative double. After a start of 1♣ – Dble – 2♣, you might make a responsive double on as little as seven points. You are only forcing the bidding to the two-level, after all.

Do you lose much by treating such a double as for take-out? Not really. It is hardly attractive to double the opponents for penalties when they have found a good fit. You will usually do at least as well by choosing trumps yourself.

The competitive double

We will end the chapter by looking at another situation where the opponents have found a fit and a penalty double will rarely be worthwhile. Look at this bidding problem:

West	West	North	East	South
♠ 9 3	–	1♠	2♦	2♠
♥ A Q 8 3	?			
♦ J 2				
♣ K J 8 7 4				

You are reluctant to pass, with 11 points facing a two-level overcall. What can you bid, though? It is hardly satisfactory to bid 3♣ on such a moderate suit. The answer is to make a take-out double. In this situation, when partner has overcalled and the third player has raised, the call is known as a 'competitive double'. It suggests tolerance for partner's suit (usually a doubleton) and length in the two unbid suits.

All options are open to your partner at his next turn. He can show a fit for one of your suits, he can rebid his own suit if that seems best, or he can pass the double for penalties. This last option is very much an exception and not at all the purpose of your double. Partner will rarely pass a competitive double at the two level. After a start of 1♠ – 2♦ – 3♠ – Dble, however, he would be more likely to conclude that the best option was to defend.

Points to remember

- In tournament play it is common to use the 'negative double'. A double of an overcall, up to the level of 3♠, is for take-out. It strongly suggests that you hold any unbid major suit(s).
- When you are playing negative doubles, the opener will usually re-open with a take-out double when left-hand opponent's overcall runs back to him. This is to cater for the situation where partner has a strong holding in the overcaller's suit but was unable to make a penalty double.

- In all types of bridge, players use the 'responsive double'. When your partner doubles a one-bid for take-out and the next player raises this to the two- or three-level, a double by the fourth player is a responsive double, for take-out.
- In tournament play, it is common to use the 'competitive double'. When your partner has overcalled, and the third player raises his partner to the two- or three-level, a double by the fourth player is 'competitive'. It suggests tolerance for partner's suit and length in the unbid suits.

Test yourself

(1) Playing negative doubles, you are sitting East and the bidding starts like this:

West	North	East	South
1♥	2♦	?	

What will you bid on the following East hands?

a ♠ Q 10 8 3	**b** ♠ J 9 3 2	**c** ♠ A 7 6
♥ 9 2	♥ A 8 4	♥ 6 5
♦ 7 5 3	♦ 10 8 6	♦ A Q 10 7 2
♣ A K J 4	♣ Q 10 4	♣ J 8 3

(2) Playing responsive doubles, you are sitting South and the bidding starts like this:

West	North	East	South
1♥	Dble	2♥	?

What will you bid on the following South hands?

a ♠ 10 3	**b** ♠ A J 9 3	**c** ♠ 7 6
♥ 9 8 2	♥ 8 4	♥ A Q J 8
♦ A J 5 3	♦ K Q 6	♦ 10 9 7 2
♣ K Q 6 4	♣ J 9 7 3	♣ Q 8 2

(3) Playing competitive doubles, you are sitting South and the bidding starts like this:

West	North	East	South
1♥	2♣	2♥	?

What will you bid on the following South hands:

a ♠ A J 10 3   b ♠ K 7 6 2   c ♠ K 9 4 2
   ♥ 8 3   ♥ 9 4   ♥ A J 10 8
   ♦ K 10 9 7 4   ♦ 10 6 5 3   ♦ J 9 7 2
   ♣ Q 4   ♣ K 10 4   ♣ 6

Answers

(1) a Double. Perfect for a negative double. You are strong
enough and have both the unbid suits.

   b 2♥. There is no need to make a take-out (negative)
double since you have already found a heart fit. In any
case, you are not quite strong enough.

   c Pass. Playing negative doubles, you have to pass initially
with a hand worth a penalty double. If the next player
passes, your partner is likely to re-open with a take-out
double, which you will pass.

(2) a Double. Perfect for a responsive double. You have
enough to bid at this level and both the minor suits. If,
instead, you held four spades you would make some bid
in that suit, expecting there to be a 4–4 fit.

   b 3♠. You expect partner to hold four spades, since this is
the 'other major suit'. A response of 2♠ would be an
underbid, suggesting around 6–9 points. With these
values you should issue a strong game invitation with a
jump to 3♠.

   c Pass. You would like to make a penalty double, yes, but
a double would be responsive (for take-out), so you do
best to pass. If the next player passes too, your partner
may well double a second time, again requesting a take-
out. You will be happy to pass the double for penalties.

(3) a Double. Just right for a competitive double.

   b 3♣. You are not strong enough for a competitive double
and have already found a club fit. Give a single raise.

   c Pass. You would like to double for penalties, perhaps,
but a double would be competitive. If partner has
3–1–3–6 shape and extra values, he may compete with a
further take-out double, which you would pass.

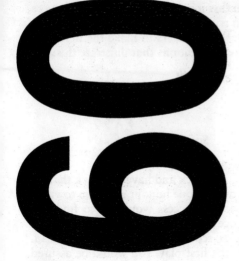

09

elimination play

In this chapter you will learn:
- how to perform an elimination play
- how to perform a loser-on-loser elimination.

Has it ever occurred to you that it is never an advantage to make the first play in a suit? You will always do at least as well, often better, if you can persuade the defenders to make the first play. Let's see a couple of single-suit positions that illustrate this.

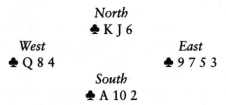

North
♦ Q 5 3

West   *East*
♦ K 10 8 2   ♦ A 9 7

South
♦ J 6 4

Suppose you need one diamond trick and have to attack the suit yourself. You would lead towards one honour and then towards the other. Your main chance of success would be to find one defender holding both the ace and king. When the cards lie as in the diagram, you would fail to score a diamond trick. If, instead, the defenders had to make the first play, you would be assured of a trick from the suit. The defender in third seat would have to rise with the ace or king and your queen-jack would then be worth a trick.

Sometimes forcing the defenders to open a suit will save you a guess. Look at this club position:

North
♣ K J 6

West   *East*
♣ Q 8 4   ♣ 9 7 5 3

South
♣ A 10 2

When you have to make the first play yourself, you can score three tricks from the suit only if you can guess which defender holds the ♣Q. When the defenders make the first play in the suit, you are certain to score three tricks.

Performing an elimination play

So, let's agree that with some holdings you would very much like the defenders to make the first play in the suit. How can you force them to do this? You do so by throwing a defender on lead after you have removed all his other possible plays. You 'eliminate' or remove from play the trumps and the other side suits, forcing the defender to play the only remaining suit (or give you a ruff-and-discard). It's not easy to imagine, perhaps, so let's look at a full deal.

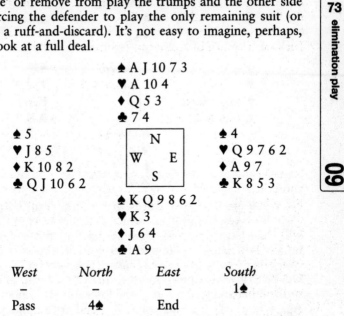

♠ A J 10 7 3
♥ A 10 4
♦ Q 5 3
♣ 7 4

♠ 5
♥ J 8 5
♦ K 10 8 2
♣ Q J 10 6 2

♠ 4
♥ Q 9 7 6 2
♦ A 9 7
♣ K 8 5 3

♠ K Q 9 8 6 2
♥ K 3
♦ J 6 4
♣ A 9

West	North	East	South
–	–	–	1♠
Pass	4♠	End	

West leads the ♣Q against your spade game. How will you play the contract?

This is the diamond suit that we saw on the previous page. As declarer, you would like to force the defenders to play diamonds for you. This can easily be done! You win the club lead and draw trumps in three rounds.

The next move is to play the king and ace of hearts and then to ruff a heart. What is the purpose of this? By removing the hearts from your own hand and the dummy (eliminating the hearts, in other words), you prevent the defenders from safely playing this suit later. If they did play a fourth round of hearts, this would give you a ruff-and-discard; you could ruff in one hand and discard a diamond loser from the other.

After drawing trumps and eliminating the heart suit, you will have reached this position:

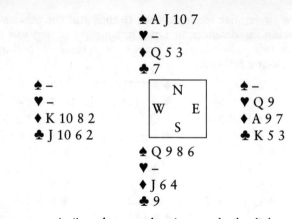

♠ A J 10 7
♥ –
♦ Q 5 3
♣ 7

♠ –
♥ –
♦ K 10 8 2
♣ J 10 6 2

N
W   E
S

♠ –
♥ Q 9
♦ A 9 7
♣ K 5 3

♠ Q 9 8 6
♥ –
♦ J 6 4
♣ 9

Now you exit (in other words, give up the lead) by playing a club. It makes no difference which defender wins this trick. He will then have only two possible plays to make. One losing option will be to make the first lead in the diamond suit, restricting your losers there to just two. The other losing option will be to give you a ruff-and-discard. You will ruff in one hand or the other and throw a diamond loser from the opposite hand. Again you will lose just two diamond tricks and make the contract.

Suppose you showed your local expert the full diagram on the previous page and asked him how he would play Four Spades on a club lead. He would reply: 'No problem there! I will draw trumps, eliminate the hearts and exit in clubs. The defenders will then have to open the diamonds or give a ruff-and-discard.'

Don't worry if elimination play is new to you and seems a bit difficult. Once you have performed a few elimination plays – and opportunities for doing so are frequent – it will soon become automatic.

Exiting in the key suit itself

On the deal we have just seen, you exited in one suit (clubs) and forced a defender to play on another (diamonds). Sometimes you exit in the key suit itself. That's what happens here:

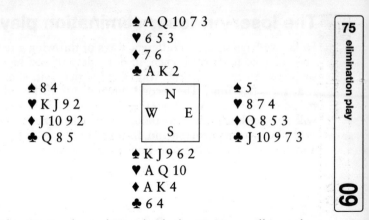

You bid to Six Spades and West leads the ♦J. How will you play the contract?

Your general plan will be to eliminate both the minor suits and then to play a heart to the ten. If West wins with the ♥J, he will have to return a heart into your ♥A-Q tenace or give you a ruff-and-discard. So, what are the steps involved in this?

You win the first trick with the ♦A and draw trumps in two rounds. You cash the ♣A-K and ruff a club in the South hand, eliminating the club suit. You then play the ♦K and ruff a diamond in dummy, eliminating the diamond suit. The lead is in dummy and these cards remain:

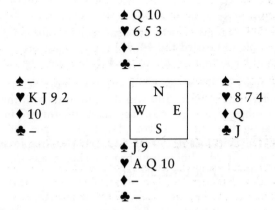

Now you play a heart to the ten. The finesse loses to the ♥J but West is end-played. He will have to play a heart into your ace-queen tenace or give you a ruff-and-discard.

The loser-on-loser elimination play

So far we have seen two different ways of throwing a defender on lead. The first arose when, in one side suit, you had a low singleton left in each hand. You exited in that suit, eliminating it at the same time. The second method was to lose the first round of the suit in which you were hoping to gain a trick. We will now look at a third method, a somewhat exotic one. You lead a loser from one hand and, instead of ruffing it, you discard a loser from some other suit. Look at this deal:

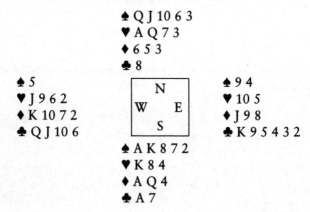

```
              ♠ Q J 10 6 3
              ♥ A Q 7 3
              ♦ 6 5 3
              ♣ 8
♠ 5                          ♠ 9 4
♥ J 9 6 2         N          ♥ 10 5
♦ K 10 7 2    W     E        ♦ J 9 8
♣ Q J 10 6       S           ♣ K 9 5 4 3 2
              ♠ A K 8 7 2
              ♥ K 8 4
              ♦ A Q 4
              ♣ A 7
```

You reach Six Spades and West leads the ♣Q. How will you plan the play?

You have two potential losers in diamonds. If the heart suit breaks 3–3, dummy's thirteenth heart will become good and you will be able to discard the ♦4. If hearts do not break 3–3, you could fall back on a finesse of the ♦Q. Is there anything better?

Indeed there is! When West holds four or more hearts, you can guarantee the contract. You win the club lead with the ace and draw trumps in two rounds. You then ruff the ♣7 in dummy, eliminating that suit. Next you play the king, ace and queen of hearts. The suit does not break 3–3, but you are pleased to see that it is West who holds four hearts. This means that you can end-play him. These cards are left:

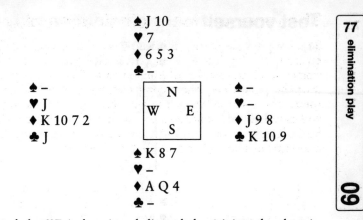

You lead the ♥7 (a loser) and discard the ♦4 (another loser). You are making what is known as a 'loser-on-loser play'. The effect of it here will be splendid. West will be left on play and will have to lead a diamond from his king into your ace-queen tenace, or give a ruff-and-discard. In both cases you will have 12 tricks and your slam.

Suppose East had started with four hearts. It would not then help you to lead the fourth heart, discarding a diamond loser. East would be left on play and could lead a diamond through the ace-queen.

Points to remember

- To perform an elimination play, you draw trumps and eliminate one or two of the side suits. You then throw a defender on lead, forcing him to make the first play in the remaining side suit or give a ruff-and-discard.

- Sometimes you throw a defender on lead on the first round of the suit in which you are hoping to gain a trick. For example, you might lead to the jack in an A-J-10 combination.

- Another possibility is to lead a loser in one suit and to discard a loser from a different suit. You gain because the defender thrown on lead will have to give you a trick with his return.

Test yourself

(1)

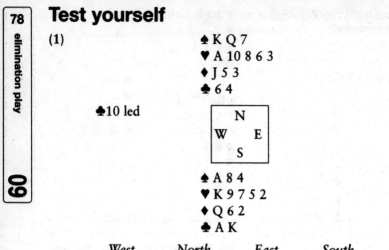

♠ K Q 7
♥ A 10 8 6 3
♦ J 5 3
♣ 6 4

♣10 led

```
      N
  W       E
      S
```

♠ A 8 4
♥ K 9 7 5 2
♦ Q 6 2
♣ A K

West	North	East	South
–	–	–	1♥
Pass	4♥	End	

West leads the ♣10 against your heart game. You win and play the ♥K, East showing out on the first round. How will you continue?

(2)

♠ Q 10 8 3 2
♥ A 9 2
♦ 7 5 3
♣ K 4

♥Q led

```
      N
  W       E
      S
```

♠ A K J 9 7 5
♥ 8
♦ A J 10
♣ A 10 3

West	North	East	South
–	–	–	1♠
Pass	4♠	Pass	6♠
End			

West leads the ♥Q against your spade slam. How will you play the contract?

Answers

(1)

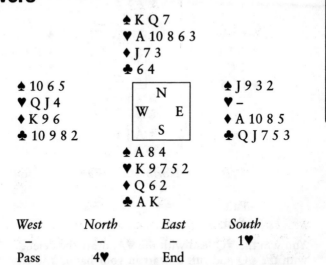

West	North	East	South
–	–	–	1♥
Pass	4♥	End	

West leads the ♣10 against Four Hearts. You win and play the ♥K, East showing out on the first round. You would like the defenders to make the first play in diamonds. Play a trump to the ace, cash your remaining club winner and continue with the three top spades. With spades and clubs now eliminated, this position has been reached:

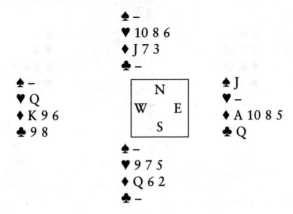

You now throw West on lead with the ♥Q. He will have to make the first play in diamonds or give you a ruff-and-discard.

(2)

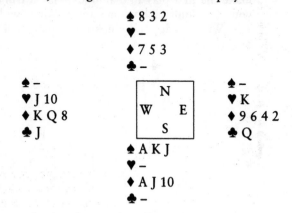

	♠ Q 10 8 3 2	
	♥ A 9 2	
	♦ 7 5 3	
	♣ K 4	
♠ 4		♠ 6
♥ Q J 10 7 4		♥ K 6 5 3
♦ K Q 8		♦ 9 6 4 2
♣ J 9 5 2		♣ Q 8 7 6
	♠ A K J 9 7 5	
	♥ 8	
	♦ A J 10	
	♣ A 10 3	

West	North	East	South
–	–	–	1♠
Pass	4♠	Pass	6♠
End			

You win the ♥Q lead with the ♥A, draw the defenders' trumps with the ♠Q and ruff a heart in your hand. You cash the king and ace of clubs and ruff a club (eliminating clubs). You ruff dummy's last heart (eliminating hearts) and return to dummy with the ♠10, leaving these cards still to be played:

	♠ 8 3 2	
	♥ –	
	♦ 7 5 3	
	♣ –	
♠ –		♠ –
♥ J 10		♥ K
♦ K Q 8		♦ 9 6 4 2
♣ J		♣ Q
	♠ A K J	
	♥ –	
	♦ A J 10	
	♣ –	

You now lead a diamond to the jack. West wins and is end-played. He must return a diamond into your tenace or give you a ruff-and-discard.

10

bidding the opponent's suit

In this chapter you will learn:
- how to show a strong raise after an enemy overcall
- how to show a strong raise of partner's overcall
- how to show a strong hand opposite a take-out double.

As you know, bids can be made in only five denominations: no-trumps and the four suits. Suppose an opponent has bid hearts. If you and your partner never make any subsequent bids in hearts yourselves, you will be greatly restricting your bidding vocabulary.

Tournament players are unwilling to restrict themselves in this way. They like to make full use of every available bid! What do you think a bid in the opponent's suit should mean? In general, it shows a strong hand of some sort and in this chapter we will see the most important uses of such bids.

Showing a strong raise after an overcall

Suppose your partner opens 1♥ and the next player overcalls 1♠. When you hold four-card heart support you would like to raise the bidding as high as you dare, to restrict the bidding space available to the opponents. When you make such a pre-emptive raise, you don't want partner to think that you have a good hand and perhaps carry the bidding to an expensive level. So, you would like to be able to tell partner, 'I have a weak hand but I am bidding high to make life difficult for the other side'. It can be done! This is the scheme of responses when your partner's opening bid has been overcalled:

West	North	East	South
1♥	1♠	?	

East responds along these lines:

2♥   three-card raise and about 5–9 points

3♥   four-card raise and about 4–8 points, pre-emptive

4♥   five-card raise and about 5–9 points, pre-emptive

2♠   sound high-card raise to at least 3♥.

As you see, on any hand that is worth a genuine game try, based on high-card values, you begin with a cue-bid in the opponent's suit.

Using this method, which is almost universal in tournament play, what would you respond (after the auction shown above) on the following East hands?

a ♠ 10 3　　　　b ♠ 9 8　　　　c ♠ A 10 6
　♥ K 8 2　　　　　♥ A J 8 4　　　　♥ Q J 8 2
　♦ 10 8 7 5　　　　♦ 10 8 6 3 2　　　♦ J 2
　♣ K J 6 4　　　　♣ 7 6　　　　　　♣ K 9 5 2

You raise to 2♥ on **a** and make a pre-emptive raise to 3♥ on **b**.
Hand **c** represents a genuine high-card raise to 3♥, so you begin
with a cue-bid of 2♠.

Perhaps you are not particularly impressed by this. You should
be! It is one of the most important developments in bidding in
the last two decades or so. When you have a good fit for partner
but little overall strength, it is important to deny your
opponents bidding space with a pre-emptive raise. By raising to
3♥ on hand **b**, for example, you rob the fourth player of the
chance to raise his partner to 2♠. If he then has to bid 3♠ on
hands that are really worth only a single raise to 2♠, as well as
those worth a sound raise to 3♠, his partner will have no
accurate picture of what strength lies opposite.

Let's look at the situation from the opener's point of view.
Suppose your opening bid is overcalled and partner shows a
sound raise, by making a cue-bid. You should sign off at the
minimum level, when you would have rejected a normal double-
raise game try (1♥ – 3♥, for example) had there been no
intervention. This is a typical auction:

West	East		West	North	East	South
♠ K J 4 3	♠ Q 10 2		1♥	2♣	3♣	Pass
♥ A Q 8 5 2	♥ K J 6 3		3♥	End		
♦ Q 6	♦ A 7 4					
♣ 9 3	♣ J 10 5					

East shows a sound high-card raise to the three-level and West
signs off. West's ♦Q-6 is worth very little. Had he held ♦K-6
instead, he would probably have rebid 4♥ instead of 3♥. Now
look at the East hand. Had his clubs been ♣K-10-5, he would
still have begun with a cue-bid (because a raise to 4♥ would
suggest a moderate hand with five-card support). However, with
13 points he would then have raised partner's 3♥ sign-off to 4♥.

Showing a strong raise of partner's overcall

Exactly the same principle applies when your partner has made an overcall. With three-card support (particularly when you hold an honour in partner's suit) you will usually give a single raise to remove bidding space from the opponents. You should raise even when your hand is quite weak. With four-card support, you should aim to raise a one-level overcall to the three-level, again even when quite weak.

This is the general scheme, when partner has overcalled:

West	North	East	South
1♦	1♠	Pass	?

Sitting South, you respond along these lines:

2♠   three-card raise and about 5–9 points

3♠   four-card raise and about 4–8 points

4♠   five-card raise and about 5–9 points

2♦   sound high-card raise to at least 2♠.

You expect partner to hold five spades for his overcall. In general, you add the number of cards you hold in support and raise to the appropriate level. With an expected eight-card fit (5 + 3) you raise to the eight-trick level and bid 2♠. With a nine-card fit (5 + 4) you raise to 3♠, and with a ten-card fit (5 + 5) you bid 4♠. With 10 points or more you will begin with a cue-bid in the opponent's suit.

After the start to the auction shown above, how would you respond on these South hands?

a ♠ K 9 4	**b** ♠ Q 10 7 2	**c** ♠ A J 5
♥ 10 5	♥ 8 4 3	♥ A 8 2
♦ 9 8 4 3	♦ 9 2	♦ 9 6
♣ Q 10 7 2	♣ K J 8 4	♣ Q 10 8 4 3

On hand **a** you raise partner's 1♠ overcall to 2♠. With hand **b**, and an expected nine-card fit, you raise pre-emptively to 3♠. Hand **c** represents a sound high-card raise to the two-level, almost to the three-level in this case, so you begin with a cue-bid of 2♦.

The cue-bid response to a take-out double

When you are responding to a take-out double you have two duties. You must choose a denomination (a trump suit or no-trumps). You must also give some idea of the strength of your hand, so that partner can judge if a game may be worth bidding. Suppose the auction starts like this:

West	North	East	South
–	1♣	Dble	Pass
?			

Sitting West, you would respond along these lines:

Pass	Long and solid clubs – this is a rare action
1♦ / 1♥ / 1♠	About 0–7 points
1NT	6–10 points and a good club stopper
2♦ / 2♥ / 2♠	8–10 points
2♣	The cue-bid shows 11+ points
2NT	11–12 points and a good club stopper
3NT	13+ points and a good club stopper
4♥/4♠	With enough for game and a five-card suit

So, you choose a trump suit at the minimum level when you hold a weak hand. With a hand of middle strength, about 8–10 points, you jump one level. When you hold upwards of 11 points but cannot tell which suit will be best, you show your general strength with a cue-bid in the enemy suit. Since this is the topic of the present section, let's see a couple of auctions that involve this particular response.

West	East	West	North	East	South
♠ K Q 8 3	♠ A J 9 2	–	–	–	1♣
♥ A J 8 2	♥ Q 3	Dble	Pass	2♣	Pass
♦ A J 6	♦ 9 5 4 2	2♥	Pass	2♠	Pass
♣ 9 3	♣ A 10 5	4♠			

East has the values to respond 2NT, but if there is a 4-4 spade fit he would like to play in that suit instead. He shows his general strength (11+ points) with a cue-bid and the two players bid their suits in ascending order until a fit is found. West shows his hearts and East shows his spades. If West were to raise to just 3♠ now, this would not be forcing. Since West holds 15 points and expects his partner to have 11 or more, he leaps to 4♠ and the best contract is reached.

West	East		West	North	East	South
♠ A Q 7 6	♠ K 9 8 4		–	–	–	3♦
♥ A J 2	♥ K 10 9 4		Dble	Pass	4♦	Pass
♦ A 5	♦ 9 6 3		4♠			
♣ J 8 6 4	♣ A 5					

East decides that his three good cards justify bidding to the game level. Should he bid 4♠ or 4♥, do you think? There is no need to guess! He shows his strength with a cue-bid of 4♦ and West will then bid his own suits up the line. In this case West does not hold four hearts and therefore rebids 4♠. Once again the best contract is reached.

Points to remember

- When you hold support for partner's suit and the auction becomes competitive, you should raise partner as high as is practical. On a hand with a moderate point-count, you will generally give a single raise when you have three-card support and a double raise with four-card support.

- Obviously, you cannot make the same bid with a weakish hand and a fairly strong hand. Any direct raises of partner's overcall tend to be pre-emptive in nature. When, instead, you have a sound game-try hand with 10 points or more, you indicate this with a cue-bid in the enemy suit.

- When you hold 11+ points opposite partner's take-out double, and no particularly long suit, you begin with a cue-bid. Both players then bid their suits upwards until a fit is found. The bidding may stop at the three-level if both players are minimum for their actions so far.

Test yourself

(1) You are sitting East, facing an opening bid, and the bidding starts like this:

West	North	East	South
1♥	2♦	?	

What will you bid on the following East hands?

a ♠ 8 5 3   b ♠ 9 6 4   c ♠ A Q 6
  ♥ A 10 9 3 2   ♥ J 8 4   ♥ K J 8 3
  ♦ 7   ♦ 10 8 6   ♦ 10 7
  ♣ Q 10 8 4   ♣ A K 9 4   ♣ J 9 3 2

(2) Now you are sitting South, facing an overcall by partner. The bidding starts like this:

West	North	East	South
1♥	2♣	Pass	?

What will you bid on the following South hands?

a ♠ K 10 5 3   b ♠ A 9 6 4   c ♠ K 8 4
  ♥ 9 8 4 2   ♥ 10 3   ♥ A J 9
  ♦ J 5   ♦ K J 6   ♦ 10 9 7 2
  ♣ K 6 4   ♣ A 10 7 3   ♣ K 8 2

(3) Still in the South seat, you now face a take-out double from your partner. The bidding starts like this:

West	North	East	South
1♥	Dble	Pass	?

How will you respond on the following South hands?

a ♠ A J 7 4   b ♠ K 8 2   c ♠ Q 3
  ♥ 10 7 3   ♥ 9 8   ♥ A Q 7 6
  ♦ K 2   ♦ A Q J 6   ♦ 10 7 4
  ♣ J 9 8 5   ♣ Q 10 7 2   ♣ K 9 8 2

Answers

(1) a 4♥. With a five-card fit, you jump to the four-level. This is what players call a 'two-way bid'. For all you know, partner may make the contract. The bid may also work well because it shuts out the player in the fourth seat. It is possible that North–South have a good spade fit, for example.

  b 2♥. With a three-card fit, you should not carry the bidding beyond the two-level unless you hold the high-card points to do so.

  c 3♦. Here you have a genuine high-card raise to the three-level. Since a direct raise to 3♥ would be pre-emptive, you must begin with a cue-bid.

(2) **a** 3♣. With three-card support including a top honour, you are keen to raise the bidding one level. As well as removing bidding space from the opener, you tell partner that you would be happy for him to lead a club if the opponents win the auction.

b 2♥. Here you have a sound high-card raise of partner's clubs. You indicate this with a cue-bid in the enemy suit.

c 2NT. When your fit is in a minor suit, the most obvious target is 3NT rather than five of a minor. Here you have a very good stopper in the opponent's suit and it is more helpful to bid 2NT rather than to make a cue-bid in the enemy suit.

(3) **a** 2♠. With a hand in the 8–10 point range you make a single jump in your preferred trump suit.

b 2♥. Here you have a strong hand but no idea which denomination will be best. You begin with a cue-bid to show the strength of your hand.

c 2NT. With 11 points and a double stopper in the opponent's suit, your best bid is 2NT.

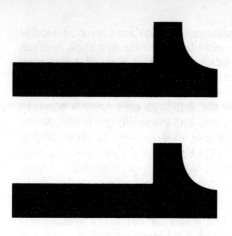

clues from the bidding

In this chapter you will learn:

- how to make deductions from the enemy bidding
- when an opponent has opened 1NT
- when an opponent has pre-empted
- when an opponent has failed to open
- when an opponent has failed to respond.

As declarer, you must gather information from every available source. The opening lead, and the play to the first trick, will tell you quite a bit about the lie of the suit that was led. Every time a player shows out of a suit subsequently, it will help you to build up a picture of the shape the defenders' hands. You may also be assisted by the signals that the defenders pass to each other. In this chapter we will look at the clues provided by a fourth source – the opponents' bidding or lack of it. Pay due attention in this area and you can avoid many a guess in the play.

When an opponent has opened 1NT

It is particularly informative when an opponent opens 1NT, showing a balanced hand and a point-count within a narrow range. Look at this deal:

```
                 ♠ 9 8 5 3
                 ♥ K J 6
                 ♦ J 6 4
                 ♣ A Q 7
   ♠ J 7                          ♠ 6 2
   ♥ 9 8 4 2          N           ♥ Q 7 5
   ♦ A K Q        W       E       ♦ 10 9 5 2
   ♣ K 10 8 4         S           ♣ 9 6 5 3
                 ♠ A K Q 10 4
                 ♥ A 10 3
                 ♦ 8 7 3
                 ♣ J 2
```

West	North	East	South
1NT	Pass	Pass	2♠
Pass	4♠	End	

West opens a weak 1NT, showing 12–14 points. You bid to 4♠ and West launches the defence by cashing the ace, king and queen of diamonds. How will you play the contract when West switches to the jack of trumps at Trick 2?

You win and draw trumps in one further round. The ♣J is covered by the king and ace and the contract is now yours if you can guess which defender holds the ♥Q. A lazy player might say to himself: 'West opened the bidding so I will finesse him for the missing queen.' A more disciplined declarer would note that West had already shown up with 9 points in diamonds, 1 point in trumps and 3 points in clubs. That is 13 points already and the ♥Q in addition would give him 15 points, too much for a weak 1NT opening. So, the correct play is to cross to the ♥K and then finesse the ♥10. East does indeed hold the ♥Q and you make the contract.

Suppose, instead, that West's 1NT opening had promised 15–17 points. Without the ♥Q he would hold only 14 points, so you would play the hand differently, finessing West for the ♥Q.

When an opponent has pre-empted

An opponent who pre-empts against you can prove a nuisance in the auction, robbing you of precious bidding space. If you end up playing the contract, however, the information provided by the pre-empt may be valuable in the play. Because the pre-empter is unusually long in his own suit, he will be correspondingly short in the other three suits. You will tend to finesse his partner for any missing honour. Look at this deal:

```
              ♠ A J 8 6
              ♥ A Q 7
              ♦ K J 7 3
              ♣ A 10
♠ 3                          ♠ Q 5 4
♥ 8 6 3          N           ♥ 10 5 4 2
♦ 6 4        W     E         ♦ Q 10 9 5
♣ K Q J 8 7 6 3     S        ♣ 5 2
              ♠ K 10 9 7 2
              ♥ K J 9
              ♦ A 8 2
              ♣ 9 4
```

West	North	East	South
3♣	Dble	Pass	4♠
Pass	6♠	End	

North–South overbid somewhat, arriving in a poor slam. How would you play this contract when West leads the ♣K?

You win with the ♣A and see that your first task is to pick up the trump suit. Normally, with nine cards between the hands, you would play to drop a missing queen. The odds in favour of this play are only 52 per cent compared with 48 per cent, however, and these are easily overturned when you know that one of the defenders is particularly long in some other suit. Here you expect West to hold seven clubs to his partner's two. Since East will then hold eleven non-club cards to West's six, he is likely to be longer than West in each of the other three suits. In particular, the odds strongly favour finessing East for the missing ♠Q.

You cash the ♠A, finesse the ♠10 successfully and draw the last trump with the ♠K. You then play three rounds of hearts, both defenders following all the way. West has indicated seven clubs with his 3♣ opening and has shown up with one spade and at least three hearts. His shape is 1–3–2–7 (or 1–4–1–7) and he can hold no more than two cards in diamonds. When you play ace and another diamond, West follows with the ♦4 and the ♦6. There is no point taking a finesse of the ♦J because West cannot hold another diamond. You rise with the ♦K in dummy, leaving these cards still to be played:

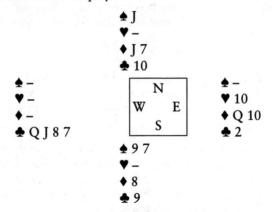

```
              ♠ J
              ♥ –
              ♦ J 7
              ♣ 10
  ♠ –                      ♠ –
  ♥ –          N           ♥ 10
  ♦ –      W       E       ♦ Q 10
  ♣ Q J 8 7        S       ♣ 2
              ♠ 9 7
              ♥ –
              ♦ 8
              ♣ 9
```

Now you play dummy's ♣10. West has to win the trick and concede a ruff-and-discard with his return. You ruff in the dummy and discard your ♦8, making the slam.

Are you thinking: 'I could never make clever plays like that'? Yes, you can! When you take the trouble to count the defenders' hands, all sorts of plays become possible.

Remember that when a player is long in one suit (perhaps he has pre-empted or overcalled), he is likely to be shorter than his partner in the other three suits. This will often affect the way that you play those suits.

When an opponent has failed to open

A player who had the chance to open the bidding but declined to do so will generally hold fewer than 12 points. If he has shown up with, say, 10 points in three suits, he is unlikely to hold the queen of the fourth suit. Inferences of this sort will often allow you to place the cards successfully. Test yourself on this deal:

```
                  ♠ 9 5 2
                  ♥ 9 7 2
                  ♦ K J 4 2
                  ♣ K 10 4
 ♠ K Q J 7      ┌──────────┐    ♠ 10 6 4 3
 ♥ Q J 8        │    N     │    ♥ 6
 ♦ Q 9 6        │ W     E  │    ♦ A 10 7 3
 ♣ 9 7 5        │    S     │    ♣ J 8 3 2
                └──────────┘
                  ♠ A 8
                  ♥ A K 10 5 4 3
                  ♦ 8 5
                  ♣ A Q 6
```

West	North	East	South
Pass	Pass	Pass	1♥
Pass	2♥	Pass	4♥
End			

West leads the ♠K against your game in hearts. You win with the ace and cash the ace and king of trumps, discovering that West began with Q-J-8 in the suit. With two certain losers in the major suits, you will now need to guess how to play the diamonds. How will you continue?

West's lead of the ♠K more or less guarantees that he also holds the ♠Q, quite possibly the ♠J as well. Since he has also shown up with ♥Q-J-x, he began with 8 or 9 points in the major suits. The ♦A in addition would have given him an opening bid of some sort, so you can place this card with East. The only chance is that West holds the ♦Q, which would leave him with 10 or 11 points, just short of an opening bid. You therefore play a diamond to the jack. This does indeed force the ace, as you were hoping, and the contract is yours.

When an opponent has failed to respond

A player who holds upwards of 6 points will generally respond to an opening one-bid in a suit. The fact that a player did not find such a response will severely limit the points that he can hold. Take the South cards on this deal:

```
              ♠ A 6 3
              ♥ K 9 5
              ♦ K Q 6 4
              ♣ Q 7 3

♠ Q 8                        ♠ 10 9 5
♥ Q J 10 2       N           ♥ A 7 6 3
♦ J 7        W       E       ♦ 8 2
♣ A K J 10 4     S           ♣ 9 6 5 2

              ♠ K J 7 4 2
              ♥ 8 4
              ♦ A 10 9 5 3
              ♣ 8
```

West	North	East	South
1♣	Pass	Pass	1♠
Pass	2♣	Pass	2♦
Pass	4♠	End	

West leads the ♣A against your spade game and switches to the ♥Q at Trick 2. East wins dummy's ♥K with the ace and returns a heart to West's ten. How will you play the contract when West persists with the ♥J at Trick 4?

You ruff in the South hand and must now pick up the trump suit to make the contract. With eight cards between the hands you would normally finesse East for the missing ♠Q, crossing to the ♠A and finessing the ♠J on the second round. Here, however, East has already shown up with the ♥A and he failed to find a response to partner's 1♣ opening. It is reasonable to deduce that West holds the ♠Q. You therefore play the ♠A and ♠K, claiming your reward when the queen falls doubleton offside.

Suppose, instead, that East had made some low-level response. You would then be inclined to place East with 6 points and would have no reason not to finesse him for the ♠Q.

Points to remember

- When you are trying to place honour cards in the defenders' hands, remember any evidence provided by the auction. A defender who opened the bidding will usually hold 12 points or more. A defender who responded will usually hold at least 6 points.
- Particularly informative bids are 1NT openings and pre-emptive openings that indicate a seven-card suit.
- Remember also the bids that were *not* made and the inferences that follow. A player who did not open, for example, will usually hold fewer then 12 points. A player who failed to respond to a one-bid will usually hold fewer than 6 points.
- By playing on the other three suits, to discover the defenders' length and high-card points there, you may find it easier to read the lie of the fourth suit.

Test yourself

(1)

     ♠ Q 5 4 2
     ♥ 9 7 2
     ♦ A Q 4
     ♣ K J 4

♥K led

```
        N
    W       E
        S
```

     ♠ K 10 9 8 6 3
     ♥ A 5
     ♦ K J 5
     ♣ 6 3

West	North	East	South
1NT	Pass	Pass	2♠
Pass	4♠	End	

West opens a 12–14 point 1NT and you end in 4♠. How will you play this contract when West leads the ♥K?

(2)

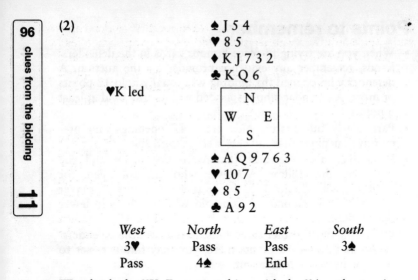

♠ J 5 4
♥ 8 5
♦ K J 7 3 2
♣ K Q 6

♥K led

♠ A Q 9 7 6 3
♥ 10 7
♦ 8 5
♣ A 9 2

West	North	East	South
3♥	Pass	Pass	3♠
Pass	4♠	End	

West leads the ♥K, East overtaking with the ♥A and returning a second round of hearts to the ten and jack. How will you play the contract when West then switches to the ♣7?

Answers

(1)

♠ Q 5 4 2
♥ 9 7 2
♦ A Q 4
♣ K J 4

♠ A J
♥ K Q J 8
♦ 9 8 6
♣ Q 9 7 5

♠ 7
♥ 10 6 4 3
♦ 10 7 3 2
♣ A 10 8 2

♠ K 10 9 8 6 3
♥ A 5
♦ K J 5
♣ 6 3

West	North	East	South
1NT	Pass	Pass	2♠
Pass	4♠	End	

West opens a 12–14 point 1NT and you end in 4♠. How will you play this contract when West leads the ♥K?

You win with the ♥A and turn your attention first to the trump suit. Since only West can possibly hold ♠A-J-6, you should lead the king on the first round of spades. West wins with the ♠A and East follows with the ♠6. When West continues with the queen and jack of hearts, you ruff the third round and draw West's last trump, the jack. You now need to guess the club suit in order to make the contract. What guess will you make?

West has shown up with 11 points in the major suits (five in spades and six in hearts). If he held the ♣A in addition, he would have a total of 15 points, which is too much for his weak 1NT opening. You should therefore lead a club towards dummy and finesse the ♣J. When this forces East's ♣A, the contract is yours.

Suppose West had opened with a strong 1NT of 15–17 points instead. He would then need the ♣A to bring his total to the required 15 points. You would play a club to dummy's king instead, again making the contract.

(2)

```
                    ♠ J 5 4
                    ♥ 8 5
                    ♦ K J 7 3 2
                    ♣ K Q 6
    ♠ 8                             ♠ K 10 2
    ♥ K Q J 9 6 4 3    N            ♥ A 2
    ♦ Q 6 4        W       E        ♦ A 10 9
    ♣ 7 5              S            ♣ J 10 8 4 3
                    ♠ A Q 9 7 6 3
                    ♥ 10 7
                    ♦ 8 5
                    ♣ A 9 2
```

West	North	East	South
3♥	Pass	Pass	3♠
Pass	4♠	End	

West leads the ♥K, East overtaking with the ♥A and returning a second round of hearts to the ten and jack. How will you play the contract when West then switches to the ♣7?

West holds seven hearts to his partner's two, so it is quite likely that East will hold more trumps than West does. You should win the club switch with the ♣K and lead the ♠J from dummy, planning to play East for ♠K-10-8-2, ♠K-10-8, ♠K-10-2 or ♠K-8-2.

Let's assume that East covers with the ♠K. You win with the ace and re-enter dummy with the ♣Q to finesse the ♠9. Your card reading proves to be valid and the finesse succeeds. You draw East's last trump with the ace and must now guess the diamond suit. Will you lead low to the jack or low to the king?

Most players would rate ♥K-Q-J-x-x-x-x and the ♦A as too much for a three-level opening, so you should play West for the ♦Q. You lead a diamond to the jack and … yes! It does force East's ace. The spade game is yours.

12

maintaining defensive communications

In this chapter you will learn:
- how to keep in touch with partner in defence
- when to hold up a high card in defence
- about ducking when partner leads your suit
- how to take stoppers in the right order.

Just as declarer has to manage communications between his own hand and the dummy, so do the defenders have to take steps to keep in touch with each other. The most important situation is when you have led a long suit against a no-trump contract and want to be able cash your winners, once the suit has been established.

Returning the right card

To enable the opening leader to read the lie of the suit, his partner must follow an agreed procedure when choosing which card to return on the second round. Look at this deal:

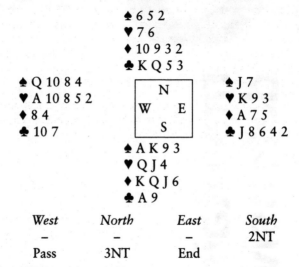

```
                    ♠ 6 5 2
                    ♥ 7 6
                    ♦ 10 9 3 2
                    ♣ K Q 5 3
    ♠ Q 10 8 4        ┌─────────┐        ♠ J 7
    ♥ A 10 8 5 2      │    N    │        ♥ K 9 3
    ♦ 8 4          W  │         │  E     ♦ A 7 5
    ♣ 10 7            │    S    │        ♣ J 8 6 4 2
                    └─────────┘
                    ♠ A K 9 3
                    ♥ Q J 4
                    ♦ K Q J 6
                    ♣ A 9
```

West	North	East	South
–	–	–	2NT
Pass	3NT	End	

Sitting West, you lead the ♥5 against 3NT. Your partner wins with the ♥K and returns the ♥9, covered by declarer's ♥Q. What will you do on this trick?

Let's see first what will happen if you win with the ♥A and play a third round of hearts to clear the suit. Declarer will win with the ♥J and play on diamonds. When your partner wins with the ♦A, he will have no heart to return. Declarer will capture East's return in some other suit and score nine tricks.

What went wrong? By capturing the second round of hearts with the ace, you lost touch with your partner. The winning defence was to play low on the second round of hearts, allowing South's ♥Q to win. When your partner subsequently took his

♦A he would have a heart to return. You would win this third round of hearts with the ace and cash two more heart winners to put 3NT one down.

If declarer had started with ♥Q-4 (instead of ♥Q-J-4) it would not be a good idea to allow him to win the second round, of course! So, you need to know what cards declarer holds in the suit. Your partner will help you to read the lie of the cards by following this rule with his lead to the second round of the suit:

When you have two cards remaining, return the higher one.

With more than two, return the original fourth-best card.

Look back to the deal on the previous page. East returned the ♥9. This told you that he had started with ♥K-9-3 (or ♥K-9 doubleton). When East has ♥K-9-3, declarer has a certain trick with his ♥Q-J-4. It is essential to duck the second round of the suit to allow your partner to cross to your ♥A later. (When partner holds a doubleton heart it is unlikely to make any difference, whatever you do.)

Let's see a deal where it would be wrong to hold up. Remember the rule above and see if you would have been able to tell, sitting West, whether to hold up your high card or not.

```
                    ♠ 8 6
                    ♥ Q 7 2
                    ♦ Q J 9 3
                    ♣ A Q 5 3
  ♠ A 10 7 5 4                          ♠ K J 3 2
  ♥ 9 8 5 3          N                  ♥ A 10 4
  ♦ 7 5          W       E              ♦ 10 4 2
  ♣ 7 4              S                  ♣ 9 8 6
                    ♠ Q 9
                    ♥ K J 6
                    ♦ A K 8 6
                    ♣ K J 10 2
```

West	North	East	South
–	–	–	1NT
Pass	3NT	End	

You lead the ♠5 and East wins with the ♠K, South following with the ♠9. East returns the ♠2 and declarer plays the ♠Q. Will you hold up or not?

East's ♠2 return looks like an original fourth-best card. In that case, declarer began with ♠Q-9 doubleton, and you must take your ace immediately. (If you don't, in fact, declarer will score eight more tricks in the minor suits and make the contract.) The only other possibility is that East began with ♠K-2 and that declarer holds ♠Q-J-9-3. In that case, your play is unlikely to make any difference. So, you should win with the ♠A and return the ♠4. The defenders will score five spade tricks and the ♥A, putting the game two down.

Was declarer more likely to hold ♠Q-9, or ♠Q-J-9-3, do you think? He was almost certain to hold the doubleton combination! Otherwise he would have no reason to waste his ♠9 at Trick 1. He would have followed with the ♠3 instead.

So, look carefully at the card that partner returns. You will often be able to work out how the suit lies and whether it is right for you to hold up your high card.

Ducking when your suit is led

One of the main reasons for bidding a good suit is that you want partner to lead it if the opponents win the auction. Suppose you overcall 1♠ on ♠A-K-J-10-5 and the player on your left becomes declarer in 3NT. Your partner leads the ♠8 and you may now have to take special steps to keep in touch with him. Let's put that spade suit into a complete deal:

```
              ♠ 7 4 2
              ♥ A 8 3
              ♦ K Q 4
              ♣ A K Q 10
 ♠ 8 6                        ♠ A K J 10 5
 ♥ J 7 5 2      N             ♥ Q 10 6
 ♦ A 9 7 3   W     E          ♦ 8 6 2
 ♣ 7 6 3        S             ♣ 8 5
              ♠ Q 9 3
              ♥ K 9 4
              ♦ J 10 5
              ♣ J 9 4 2
```

West	North	East	South
–	1♣	1♠	1NT
Pass	3NT	End	

You overcall 1♠ and your partner leads the ♠8 against the eventual 3NT contract. How will you defend in the East seat?

It may seem natural to win with the ♠K and to clear the spade suit by continuing with the ♠A and ♠J, forcing out South's ♠Q. This defence will not beat the contract, however. With only seven tricks on top, declarer will have to set up two tricks in diamonds. When your partner wins with the ♦A he will have no spade to return! Declarer will capture whatever other suit West returns and score nine tricks for his contract.

To keep in touch with partner you must not play the king or ace of spades on the first trick. You should play the ♠10 instead, letting South score his spade trick at a moment that suits you. Do you see the point of defending in this way? You leave your partner with a spade in his hand. When declarer eventually plays on diamonds, your partner will rise immediately with the ♦A and return his remaining spade. The defenders will score four spade tricks and one diamond trick to beat the contract.

Sometimes you would make this ducking play even with the ace-king-queen in your suit. Suppose you have overcalled 1♠ and South is now in 3NT with the spade suit lying like this:

North
♠ 8 4

West   *East*
♠ 7 2   ♠ A K Q 10 5

South
♠ J 9 6 3

Partner leads the ♠7. It is fairly obvious that South must hold a spade stopper, in order to justify his no-trump bid. Play the ♠10 and let him win his spade trick immediately. Then your partner will have a spade to return if he gains the lead.

Taking stoppers in the right order

Sometimes declarer has two stoppers to knock out, before he can score the nine tricks that he needs for 3NT. This will give you more time, as defenders, to establish your own suit. It may be important, though, that you take your stoppers in the right order. You will want to leave an entry to the hand with the long cards in the defenders' suit. This deal illustrates the situation:

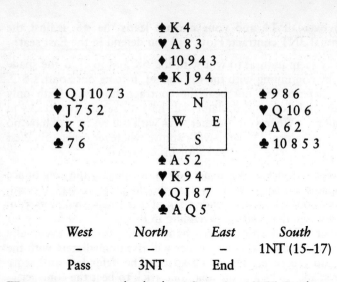

West	North	East	South
–	–	–	1NT (15–17)
Pass	3NT	End	

West, your partner, leads the ♠Q against 3NT. Declarer can count eight top tricks and sees that he will have to set up the diamond suit in order to score a ninth trick. Correctly, he allows the ♠Q to win the first trick and wins the next round of spades with dummy's king. (If spades had been 6–2 between the defenders' hands, declarer's hold-up would have left East with no spade to play.)

Now comes the key moment for the defence. Declarer leads the ♦3 from dummy. How will you defend in the East seat?

To beat the contract, you must rise immediately with the ♦A and return your remaining spade. This will clear the spade suit and partner will then have two spade tricks to cash when he wins the next round of diamonds with the king. Suppose you are not awake and play low on the first round of diamonds. Your partner wins with the ♦K and clears the spade suit but he will never gain the lead to cash his two winners. When you win the next round of diamonds with the ace, you will have no spade to play.

Some players are worried about rising with the ♦A on deals like this, in case declarer holds ♦K-J-x-x and has a guess to make in the suit. That's possible, but you still won't beat the contract by playing low on the first round of diamonds. Say that declarer plays the ♦J to partner's ♦Q and the spades are cleared. Again you will have no spade to play when you win with the ♦A.

Points to remember

- When you are returning the suit that partner has led, lead the top card when you have two cards remaining and the original fourth best from any longer holding.

- When you have led from a long suit headed by an honour, it may be right to hold up the high card on the second round. By leaving partner with a card in the suit, you will benefit if he gains the lead later and can cross to your high card. You will then be able to cash your established winners.

- When the defenders hold two stoppers in declarer's suits it may be important to take them in the right order. You will want to preserve the high card that will serve as an entry to the long cards in the defenders' main suit.

Test yourself

(1)

```
              ♠ A 7 6 4
              ♥ Q 7
              ♦ A K 5
              ♣ 9 8 7 2
  ♠ Q 8 2         ┌─────────┐
  ♥ A 10 8 5 3    │    N    │
  ♦ 8 7 4         │ W     E │
  ♣ 6 4           │    S    │
                  └─────────┘
```

West	North	East	South
–	–	–	1♣
Pass	1♠	Pass	1NT (12–14)
Pass	3NT	End	

Sitting West, you lead the ♥5. The ♥7 is played from dummy, covered by East's ♥9 and declarer's ♥K. Declarer crosses to dummy with the ♦A and leads the ♣2. East wins with the ♣K and returns the ♥6, South playing the ♥4. How will you defend from this point?

(2)

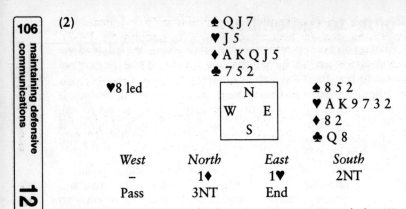

```
                        ♠ Q J 7
                        ♥ J 5
                        ♦ A K Q J 5
                        ♣ 7 5 2

♥8 led          ┌─────────────┐      ♠ 8 5 2
                │      N      │      ♥ A K 9 7 3 2
                │  W       E  │      ♦ 8 2
                │      S      │      ♣ Q 8
                └─────────────┘
```

West	North	East	South
–	1♦	1♥	2NT
Pass	3NT	End	

Your partner, West, leads the ♥8 against 3NT and the ♥J is played from dummy. What is your plan for the defence?

Answers

(1)

```
                        ♠ A 7 6 4
                        ♥ Q 7
                        ♦ A K 5
                        ♣ 9 8 7 2

♠ Q 8 2         ┌─────────────┐      ♠ J 10 5
♥ A 10 8 5 3    │      N      │      ♥ 9 6 2
♦ 8 7 4         │  W       E  │      ♦ J 10 6 3
♣ 6 4           │      S      │      ♣ A K 3
                └─────────────┘
                        ♠ K 9 3
                        ♥ K J 4
                        ♦ Q 9 2
                        ♣ Q J 10 5
```

West	North	East	South
–	–	–	1♣
Pass	1♠	Pass	1NT (12–14)
Pass	3NT	End	

Sitting West, you lead the ♥5 against 3NT. The ♥7 is played from dummy, covered by East's ♥9 and declarer's ♥K. Declarer crosses to dummy with the ♦A and leads the ♣2. East wins with the ♣K and returns the ♥6, South playing the ♥4. How will you defend from this point?

If East held the ♥J he would have played it at Trick 1, instead of the ♥9. So, declarer began with ♥K-J-4 (or possibly ♥K-J-4-2). You should allow the ♥K to win, retaining your ♥A as an entry. You expect East to hold the ♣A, because his ♣K won the first round of the suit. When East gains the lead with the ♣A you want him to have a heart to return.

When you duck the second round of hearts, declarer has no option but to play another club. East wins with the ♣A and returns the ♥2. You can now score three heart tricks to put the contract one down.

(2)

```
                    ♠ Q J 7
                    ♥ J 5
                    ♦ A K Q J 5
                    ♣ 7 5 2
♠ K 9 6 3                              ♠ 8 5 2
♥ 8 6           N                      ♥ A K 9 7 3 2
♦ 7 6 4      W     E                   ♦ 8 2
♣ K 9 6 4          S                   ♣ Q 8
                    ♠ A 10 4
                    ♥ Q 10 4
                    ♦ 10 9 3
                    ♣ A J 10 3
```

West	North	East	South
–	1♦	1♥	2NT
Pass	3NT	End	

Your partner, West, leads the ♥8 against 3NT and the ♥J is played from dummy. What is your plan for the defence?

Suppose you win dummy's ♥J with the ♥K. Whether you play the ♥A next or a low heart, the link with your partner will be broken. When declarer takes a losing spade finesse, seeking the extra trick that he needs, your partner will win with the ♠K but will have no heart to return. Declarer can win his switch and score an easy nine tricks.

To keep in touch with your partner, you must retain your two heart honours, allowing the ♥J to win. The best card to play is an encouraging ♥9. Declarer now has eight top tricks (one heart, five diamonds and two black aces). He will no doubt take the spade finesse. Unfortunately for him, West will win with the ♠K and return his remaining heart. You will enjoy five heart tricks, putting the game two down.

It's possible that your partner has only one heart, South holding
♥Q-10-6-4. In that case you and your partner cannot keep in
touch however you defend and the contract will surely be made.
When you need the cards to lie in a particular way to give you
a chance of beating the contract (here you need West to hold
two hearts), always assume that they do indeed lie that way.
Some chance is better than none!

13

playing a
cross-ruff

When you are playing in a suit contract, it is quite common to take a ruff or two in the dummy and then to draw trumps in your hand. In this chapter we will look at a slightly unusual way of playing a contract. When you have a side-suit shortage in your own hand as well as in the dummy, it may be best to take ruffs in both hands. This style of play is known as a cross-ruff. You never actually draw trumps and the defenders will usually end up with more trumps than you!

How to play a cross-ruff

Let's see an example of this style of play straight away.

```
                  ♠ A Q 10 2
                  ♥ A 9 5 4 2
                  ♦ 7 6 4
                  ♣ 7
    ♠ 8 7                         ♠ 6 5 3
    ♥ Q 6          N              ♥ K J 10 7 3
    ♦ K J 5 2   W     E           ♦ Q 10
    ♣ Q 10 9 8 4     S            ♣ K 5 3
                  ♠ K J 9 4
                  ♥ 8
                  ♦ A 9 8 3
                  ♣ A J 6 2
```

West	North	East	South
–	–	–	1♣
Pass	1♥	Pass	1♠
Pass	3♠	Pass	4♠
End			

West leads the ♠8 against your spade game. How will you play the contract?

You have only three winners in the side suits (the three aces). If you can add seven trump tricks, this will bring your total to ten. You win the first trick with the ♠A in dummy and must now aim to score all six of your remaining trumps separately. You cash the ♥A and ruff a heart with the ♠9. You then play the ♦A, scoring the one diamond trick that you need, and follow with the ♣A. Next you ruff a club with dummy's only low trump, the ♠2, which gives you six tricks in the bag. A heart ruff with the jack is followed by a club ruff with the queen, a heart ruff with the king and a final club ruff with the ace. Since the last four ruffs were taken with master trumps, there was no risk of an overruff by the defenders. Ten tricks are duly made and the game is yours.

One point to remember is that you will normally ruff with low trumps at the start of the hand, when the risk of an overruff is minimal. Later in the hand, you can ruff with master trumps and will not need to worry if a defender is out of the suit being ruffed.

Cashing side-suit winners before the cross-ruff

On many cross-ruff deals it is essential to cash all your side-suit winners before embarking on the ruffing. If you fail to do so, the defenders may discard their cards in one of the suits and then ruff your winners. It's not easy to visualize, perhaps, so let's see a deal that illustrates the situation.

```
                    ♠ 2
                    ♥ Q J 9 3
                    ♦ K 7 5
                    ♣ A J 7 5 2
    ♠ 6 3                         ♠ K Q 10 9 5
    ♥ 10 6 4 2        N           ♥ 7
    ♦ 9 8         W       E       ♦ Q J 4 3 2
    ♣ K Q 10 8 4      S           ♣ 6 3
                    ♠ A J 8 7 4
                    ♥ A K 8 5
                    ♦ A 10 6
                    ♣ 9
```

West	North	East	South
–	–	–	1♠
Pass	2♣	Pass	2♥
Pass	4♥	Pass	6♥
End			

South's final bid was somewhat exuberant, it's true, but how would you play the heart slam when West leads the ♣K?

You have four winners in the side suits. If you can add eight trump tricks, by ruffing four spades in the dummy and four clubs in your hand, this will bring the total to twelve. Suppose you win the club lead with dummy's ace and begin to cross-ruff in the black suits immediately. When you lead the third round of spades, West will take the opportunity to discard one of his diamonds. You will go down! You will not be able to score the two diamond tricks that you need.

After winning the club lead, the first thing you should do is to cash the ace and king of diamonds ('before the rats get at them', as bridge players say). That done, you play the ♠A and ruff a spade with the ♥3. You then ruff a club in your hand with the ♥5. As before, you are taking the early ruffs with low trumps, while the risk of an overruff is minimal.

When you lead another spade, West has no cards left in the suit. He cannot make a damaging discard of a diamond, as before, because you have already cashed your two diamond tricks. It won't help him to ruff, since you would overruff in the dummy, so he will doubtless throw a club. You ruff with dummy's ♥9 and ruff another club with the ♥8 as East shows out. The contract is now yours. Dummy has the ♥Q-J remaining and you have the ♥A-K. You make these master trumps separately by continuing to cross-ruff the two black suits. Twelve tricks are soon before you.

Points to remember

- When you have a side-suit shortage in both hands the best play may be a cross-ruff. You plan to score the trumps in both hands separately, by taking ruffs in two suits.
- When playing a cross-ruff you should usually score the early ruffs with low trumps, when the risk of an overruff is minimal. The later ruffs can then be taken with higher trumps, perhaps master trumps.
- Before embarking on a cross-ruff, you should cash the side-suit winners that you need. If you fail to do this, the defenders may discard as you cross-ruff and later be in a position to ruff your intended side-suit winners.

Test yourself

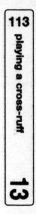

(1)

         ♠ K 9 7 3
         ♥ J 10 9 5
         ♦ A 9 7 4
         ♣ 7

♦Q led

```
        N
    W       E
        S
```

         ♠ A 5 4
         ♥ A K Q 4
         ♦ 3
         ♣ J 10 5 3 2

West	North	East	South
–	–	–	1♣
Pass	1♦	Pass	1♥
Pass	3♥	Pass	4♥
End			

West leads the ♦Q. How will you play the heart game?

(2)

         ♠ 5
         ♥ A K 2
         ♦ K Q 9 5
         ♣ A J 9 6 3

♥10 led

```
        N
    W       E
        S
```

         ♠ A J 8 7 3
         ♥ Q J 3
         ♦ A J 10 4
         ♣ 5

West	North	East	South
–	–	–	1♠
Pass	2♣	Pass	2♦
Pass	4NT	Pass	5♥
Pass	6♦	End	

West leads the ♥10 against your small slam. How will you plan the play?

Answers

(1)

```
                    ♠ K 9 7 3
                    ♥ J 10 9 5
                    ♦ A 9 7 4
                    ♣ 7
  ♠ J 6                              ♠ Q 10 8 2
  ♥ 8 6          ┌─────────────┐     ♥ 7 3 2
  ♦ Q J 10 6     │      N      │     ♦ K 8 5 2
  ♣ A Q 9 6 4    │  W       E  │     ♣ K 8
                 │      S      │
                 └─────────────┘
                    ♠ A 5 4
                    ♥ A K Q 4
                    ♦ 3
                    ♣ J 10 5 3 2
```

West	North	East	South
–	–	–	1♣
Pass	1♦	Pass	1♥
Pass	3♥	Pass	4♥
End			

West leads the ♦Q against your game in hearts. How will you play the contract?

You win with dummy's ♦A and see that you have three winners in the side suits. If you can score seven trump tricks (one round of trumps and six trumps scored separately), this will bring your total to ten. Since you will need to ruff clubs in the dummy, the next move is to lead dummy's singleton club. Let's say that the defenders win and return a trump. What then?

You win with the ♥A and cash two rounds of spades, making sure of your tricks in the side suits before the defenders have any chance to discard spades. You then ruff a diamond with the ♥4. Your remaining five trumps (♥J-10-9 in the dummy and ♥K-Q in your hand) are all masters. You can therefore cross-ruff clubs and diamonds without fear of an overruff.

As on other deals in this chapter, a trump lead would have been effective, cutting down your potential ruffs. There was no pressing reason for West to lead a trump and most players would have led the ♦Q.

(2)

```
                        ♠ 5
                        ♥ A K 2
                        ♦ K Q 9 5
                        ♣ A J 9 6 3
    ♠ K Q 9 6 2         ┌─────────┐         ♠ 10 4
    ♥ 10 9 8 6 4        │    N    │         ♥ 7 5
    ♦ 7                 │ W     E │         ♦ 8 6 3 2
    ♣ 7 4               │    S    │         ♣ K Q 10 8 2
                        └─────────┘
                        ♠ A J 8 7 3
                        ♥ Q J 3
                        ♦ A J 10 4
                        ♣ 5
```

West	North	East	South
–	–	–	1♠
Pass	2♣	Pass	2♦
Pass	4NT	Pass	5♥
Pass	6♦	End	

West leads the ♥10. How will you plan the play?

A successful cross-ruff will give you eight trump tricks. If you can add four side-suit tricks, this will be enough for your small slam. So, the two black aces and just *two* heart tricks will suffice. You should therefore cash a second heart trick immediately, before one of the defenders (East on the lay-out shown) has a chance to discard his hearts.

With two heart tricks taken, you cash the black-suit aces and take your first two ruffs, one in each black suit, with low trumps. You can then take six more ruffs with master trumps, making the slam.

Do you see what would go wrong if you mistakenly attempted to cash three rounds of hearts? East would ruff the third heart and might then return a trump. You would then go down, no longer able to score the eight trump tricks that you need.

(Suppose you bid all the way to 7♦ instead. You would then need five winners in the side-suits to go with your eight trump tricks. You would have to risk cashing three rounds of hearts at the start of the play.)

14

transfer responses

In this chapter you will learn:
- transfer responses when partner opens 1NT
- transfer responses when partner overcalls 1NT
- transfer responses when partner opens 2NT
- when you should 'break the transfer'.

Nearly all tournament players use 'transfer responses' when partner has opened 1NT. What does that mean?

Transfer responses to 1NT

2♦ shows at least five hearts and asks opener to rebid 2♥.
2♥ shows at least five spades and asks opener to rebid 2♠.

What is the point of such a method? There are two big advantages. The first is that the 1NT opener will be able to play any contract in responder's five-card major. His hand will be hidden from view and his honour holdings will be protected from the opening lead. The second advantage is that after a start of 1NT – 2♦ – 2♥, responder has a second chance to bid. He can continue with a further bid, such as 2NT, 3♣ or 3NT, having already shown five hearts.

(The examples in this chapter will assume that a 12–14 point weak 1NT is being used. If your preference is to use the 15–17 point strong 1NT, this will not affect the meaning of any of the sequences at all. You should just mentally add a king to the opening bidder's hand and subtract a king from the responder's hand.)

So, let's see some examples of transfer bids in action. The first situation is where responder is weak and wants to sign off in his long major suit.

West	East		West	East
♠ A 9 3 2	♠ 7 4		1NT	2♦
♥ K 5 2	♥ A J 8 4 3		2♥	
♦ Q J 7	♦ 10 6 5			
♣ K 10 4	♣ Q 8 2			

If transfer bids were not being used, East would have signed off in 2♥ and played the contract himself. Playing transfers, he responds 2♦ instead. The opener rebids 2♥, as requested, and East passes. Note that West's 2♥ bid does not indicate three-card heart support. He would have to make the same rebid even if he held only two hearts.

Since bidding 2♦ forces the opener to rebid 2♥, the responder has the chance to give a second description of his hand. For example, if he continues with 2NT this will show the values to invite game:

West	East	West	East
♠ K 2	♠ J 8 4	1NT	2♦
♥ A 10 4	♥ K Q 8 6 5	2♥	2NT
♦ Q 9 8 3	♦ A J 5	4♥	
♣ K Q 6 3	♣ 10 2		

East's sequence passes two messages to his partner: a) 'I have five hearts' and b) 'I am strong enough to invite game but not to insist on it'. West can now place the final contract. With a minimum 1NT opening, he would pass 2NT (with only two hearts) or sign off in 3♥ (with three hearts). With two hearts and a maximum opening, he would raise to 3NT. With four hearts, or three hearts and a maximum opening, he would bid 4♥.

Suppose East had held the ♠A instead of the ♠J on that last hand. What would he have rebid? He would have said 3NT at his second turn, asking partner to choose between 3NT and 4♥.

With six trumps and game-try values, responder can rebid in the trump suit:

West	East	West	East
♠ 9 2	♠ K Q 8 7 6 3	1NT	2♥
♥ K J 7 3	♥ A 5	2♠	3♠
♦ A 10 7	♦ J 6 3		
♣ K J 9 5	♣ 8 2		

East shows six spades and the values to invite a game. West has only two low spades and a minimum 12-count, so he declines the invitation.

When the responder has the values for game, at least, he may bid a new suit on the second round:

West	East	West	East
♠ 8 2	♠ A Q 9 7 2	1NT	2♥
♥ A Q 7	♥ K 5	2♠	3♦
♦ K J 9 3	♦ A Q 10 4	4♦	6♦
♣ Q J 9 5	♣ A 7		

East shows five spades and (at least) four diamonds, with game-forcing values. West raises the diamonds and East bids a small slam in that suit. Suppose, instead, that East held the same shape but only 13 points. If there were no spade fit, he would rather play in no-trumps than diamonds. It follows that he should not even offer the diamond suit. He should rebid 3NT at his second turn, asking partner to choose between spades and no-trumps.

Transfers opposite a 1NT overcall

When partner has overcalled 1NT, it is a good idea to use exactly the same conventional responses (Stayman and transfer bids) as you would opposite a 1NT opening.

West	East	West	North	East	South
♠ A Q 9	♠ 4 3	–	–	–	1♠
♥ Q 7	♥ K 10 9 7 2	1NT	Pass	2♦	Pass
♦ K J 8 2	♦ A 9 3	2♥	Pass	3NT	
♣ A 10 6 4	♣ K 7 3				

East shows a five-card heart suit and the values for game. Since West has only two-card heart support, he opts to pass 3NT.

Transfers opposite a 2NT opening

A similar method is used opposite an opening bid of 2NT (or when the bidding has started 2♣ – 2♦ – 2NT):

Transfer responses to 2NT

3♦ shows at least five hearts and asks opener to rebid 3♥.
3♥ shows at least five spades and asks opener to rebid 3♠.

The advantages are the same as before. The opener will play the contract, with his values hidden from view and his tenaces protected from the opening lead. Also, responder will have the chance to make a second descriptive bid. Look at this typical sequence:

West	East	West	North	East	South
♠ A Q 7	♠ J 9 6 5 2	2NT	Pass	3♥	Pass
♥ A 7	♥ 8 5 4	3♠	Pass	3NT	Pass
♦ K Q 9 4	♦ A J 3	4♠			
♣ K Q J 3	♣ 9 5				

East shows a five-card spade suit with his transfer response and continues with 3NT to offer the opener a choice of game contracts. With three-card spade support, the opener chooses to play in partner's suit.

Breaking the transfer

When the opener has four-card trump support and an upper-range hand, he should bid one level higher than normal. This is known as 'breaking the transfer'. One advantage is that game may now be reached when responder was not quite strong enough to make a try himself. That's what happens here:

West	East		West	East
♠ Q 10 7 3	♠ J 4		1NT	2♦
♥ A 8 5 2	♥ K Q 9 7 3		3♥	4♥
♦ K 2	♦ A 9 6 4			
♣ A J 4	♣ 7 5			

With just 10 points and a five-card suit, East would have passed a rebid of 2♥. When partner shows four-card heart support and an upper-range opening, East raises to game.

Similarly, the knowledge that partner has a particularly good fit for your major suit may help you to bid a slam.

Other responses to 1NT

Some tournament players use 2♠ as a transfer response showing five clubs and 2NT as transfer response showing five diamonds. That is beyond the scope of this book. For the moment, it is best to start with a Stayman response on strong hands that contain a five-card minor. You can then bid the minor on the second round. Such a rebid is forcing to game.

West	East		West	East
♠ A J 8 5	♠ Q 4		1NT	2♣
♥ J 10 6	♥ A K 7 5		2♠	3♣
♦ A Q 4	♦ K 3		3NT	
♣ 9 7 2	♣ K Q 10 8 3			

You begin with 2♣, hoping to uncover a heart fit. When partner denies a heart fit by responding 2♠, you continue with the natural and forcing 3♣, showing at least five clubs. West has no special fit for clubs, so he signs off in 3NT and you have no more to say.

An immediate jump response at the three-level shows at least a six-card suit and the possibility of a slam. When the opener's hand is suitable for a slam, he should indicate this by making a cue-bid (showing where he holds an ace or king).

West	East	West	East
♠ A 8 7 5	♠ K 4	1NT	3♥
♥ K 10 6	♥ A Q J 9 8 3	3♠	4NT
♦ A 9 6 2	♦ K 7	5♣	6♥
♣ Q 2	♣ K J 8		

East shows a six-card heart suit and suggests a slam. With three-card heart support, a ruffing value and some useful honour cards, West accepts the try by cue-bidding his ♠ A. East bids Roman Key-card Blackwood and the excellent small slam is reached.

Points to remember

- In tournament play, most players use transfer responses to 1NT openings and overcalls. A 2♦ response shows five hearts and asks the opener to rebid 2♥. A 2♥ response shows five spades and the opener should rebid 2♠.
- Responder may follow his transfer bid with a further descriptive bid on the next round.
- Transfer bids are also used opposite a 2NT opening (or after a start of 2♣ – 2♦ – 2NT).
- With four-card support and maximum for his bid, the opener may 'break the transfer' by rebidding one level higher than normal.

Test yourself

(1) You are playing Stayman and transfers and your partner has opened a 12–14 point 1NT. What is your bidding plan, as responder, on the following hands?

a ♠ Q 10 8 3 2	**b** ♠ K 3	**c** ♠ A K 10 8 6
♥ 9 2	♥ A Q J 7 4	♥ 5
♦ K 5 3	♦ 10 8	♦ A K J 2
♣ A 6 2	♣ Q J 4 3	♣ K 8 4

(2) Again your partner has opened a 12–14 point 1NT. What is your bidding plan on these responding hands?

a ♠ 3	**b** ♠ K J 9 3	**c** ♠ 9 6
♥ A J 8 2	♥ 8 4	♥ A Q J 9 6 2
♦ K Q 3	♦ A Q 10 7 6	♦ 10 7
♣ A K 6 4 2	♣ Q 7	♣ A 8 2

(3) Your partner opens 2NT, showing 20–22 points. What is your bidding plan on these responding hands?

a ♠ 7
   ♥ K 10 8 2
   ♦ Q 6 2
   ♣ A Q J 4 2

b ♠ Q J 9 3 2
   ♥ 10 8 4
   ♦ K 8 7 2
   ♣ 7

c ♠ 9 8 6
   ♥ Q 9 6 5 2
   ♦ 10 7 4 2
   ♣ 8

Answers

(1) **a** Respond 2♥ and pass 2♠. Even if partner breaks the transfer, rebidding 3♠, you should still pass.

b With 13 points, you should respond 2♦ and continue with 3NT on the next round to offer partner a choice of games. You are not strong enough to introduce the club suit because an 11-trick game will probably be too high on these values.

c Respond 2♥ and rebid 3♦, showing a strong hand with five spades and at least four diamonds.

(2) **a** Begin with a Stayman 2♣. Unless partner responds 2♥, giving you a 4–4 heart fit, continue with 3♣.

b With only 12 points, you are not strong enough to consider playing in 5♦. Use Stayman to discover if there is a 4–4 spade fit. If partner rebids 2♦ or 2♥, bid 3NT next. (The sequence 1NT – 2♣ – 2♥ – 3NT shows four spades, since otherwise you would have no reason to bid Stayman. Partner should therefore bid 4♠ with four cards in both majors.)

c Your hand is strong enough to venture a game in hearts. Begin with a 2♦ transfer and rebid 4♥. By making partner the declarer you avoid a lead through his potential spade and diamond tenaces.

(3) **a** Begin with a Stayman 3♣. Unless partner responds 3♥, when you will have a 4–4 heart fit, continue with 4♣ (natural and forcing).

b With only 6 points, you are not strong enough to consider playing in 5♦. Begin with 3♥, to show five spades, and rebid 3NT to offer a choice of games.

c You do not have enough for game, but 3♥ should be a better contract than 2NT. So, respond 3♦, intending to pass 3♥. If partner has a great heart fit, he may break the transfer, rebidding 4♥. In that case the game may well be made.

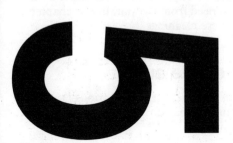

15

safety plays

In this chapter you will learn:
- how to calculate the best play in a suit
- how the best play may vary according to the tricks needed
- when you should avoid the 'normal play'
- how the best play may vary according to the lie of other suits.

What does the term 'safety play' mean? Depending on the context it can have various meanings. It can mean, 'a way of playing the contract that guarantees its success'. This is also called a '100 per cent safety play'. It can also mean 'the way of playing a contract that will give you the best chance of making it'. Finally, the term can simply mean 'the best way to play a particular suit'. As we will see shortly, this may well depend on the number of tricks that you need from the suit. In this chapter we will see examples of all these meanings.

Safety plays in a single suit

Let's look first at the play of a single suit, with various honour combinations in the two hands. What do you think is the best way to play this diamond suit?

North

♦ K J 7 5

South

♦ A 6 2

The correct answer is, 'It depends on how many tricks I need from the suit!' Suppose you need four diamond tricks to make the contract. This can be done only when West holds ♦Q-x-x. You play the ♦A on the first round and finesse the ♦J on the second round. When the perfect lie does occur, the finesse will win and the ♦K will drop West's ♦Q on the third round. You will have your four tricks from the suit.

Next, suppose that you need only three diamond tricks to make the contract. How should you play the suit then? If you follow the same line (♦A first and then finesse the ♦J), you will make at least three tricks in these three cases:

a when West holds the ♦Q
b when diamonds break 3–3
c when East holds a singleton ♦Q

A better play, when aiming for three tricks, is to cash the ♦K and ♦A and then to lead towards the ♦J. You will still succeed in cases **a**, **b** and **c** but you will add:

d when East holds a doubleton ♦Q

When only three diamond tricks are needed to make the contract, you should follow this second line. By doing so, you will give yourself the best possible chance of making the contract. You give up the chance for four diamond tricks, yes, but an overtrick is not worth very much. You must always maximize your chance of making the contract. A bridge player would say: 'The safety play for three diamond tricks is to cash the king and ace and then lead towards the jack.'

There are many suit combinations that offer you the chance of making a safety play. Before we consider the general question of how you can work out the best plays for yourself, let's see a few more suit combinations.

North
♣ K J 7 5

West   *East*
♣ Q   ♣ 10 8 6 3

South
♣ A 9 4 2

When you need four club tricks from this North–South combination, you should begin with a low club from the South hand, intending to finesse dummy's jack. You will score four tricks when West holds ♣Q, ♣Q-x or ♣Q-x-x. Note that it would not be correct to cash the ♣A on the first round, before finessing the ♣J. You would then fail to score four tricks when West held a singleton ♣Q. By leading low on the first round, you can win West's singleton ♣Q with the ♣K, continue with the ♣J and finesse the ♣9 on the third round.

How would you play the same combination if you needed only three club tricks?

North
♣ K J 7 5

West   *East*
♣ 10 8 6 3   ♣ Q

South
♣ A 9 4 2

If you make the same play that is recommended when seeking four club tricks (low to the ♣J on the first round), you would score only two club tricks when the suit lies as in this second diagram. The safety play for three club tricks (a 100% safety play, in fact) is to cash the ♣K on the first round and to lead towards the South hand, intending to finesse the ♣9 on the second round. When East holds ♣Q-10-8-x, you will score three club tricks, whether or not East decides to play the 10 on the second round. If, instead, West held ♣Q-10-8-x, East would show out on the second round. You would rise with the ♣A and lead back towards the ♣J on the third round, again making the three tricks you required.

It may all seem a bit complicated, the first time you study a particular combination like this. When you have played bridge for a while, such holdings become familiar and you can easily remember the correct play.

Many safety plays involve testing for a key defensive honour to fall before taking a finesse (as we saw with our first example, A-x-x opposite K-J-x-x). Here is another one:

North
♦ A Q 6 2

South
♦ 7 5 4

To make 3NT, let's say, you need just two diamond tricks. You have adequate protection in the other suits, so you can choose your play in diamonds. Suppose you give the matter little thought and finesse the ♦Q on the first round. You will make the required two diamond tricks in just two situations:

a when West holds the ♦K
b when diamonds break 3–3

Can you see a better way to play the combination? You must try to make two tricks in a third situation, when East holds a doubleton ♦K. Suppose the suit lies like this:

North
♦ A Q 6 2

West   *East*
♦ J 9 8 3   ♦ K 10

South
♦ 7 5 4

If you finesse on the first round, you will make only one diamond trick. The correct safety play for two tricks is to duck the first round, play the ace on the second round and then lead towards the queen on the third round. You still make two tricks in cases **a** and **b** above. You achieve your objective also when East holds a doubleton (or singleton) king.

From these examples you can begin to see how to calculate the best play with an unfamiliar combination. If two possible lines come to mind, you count how many defensive holdings each one picks up. Here the first line picked up two combinations (♦K onside or diamonds 3–3). The second line also picked up further combinations (♦K-x or single ♦K offside) and was therefore a better prospect.

When you should avoid the normal play

On many hands you cannot calculate the best way to play a combination merely by looking at that particular suit in isolation. You must consider the whole deal, in particular whether one of the defenders cannot be allowed to gain the lead. To illustrate the point, we will look at two 3NT contracts that both feature the same diamond suit. This is the first of them:

```
                    ♠ 7 6
                    ♥ K 9 6
                    ♦ A J 8 7 2
                    ♣ K 6 5
  ♠ K J 9 4 2                      ♠ Q 8 5
  ♥ Q 7 2          N              ♥ J 10 4 3
  ♦ 10 9 4      W     E           ♦ Q 3
  ♣ J 4            S              ♣ Q 9 8 2
                    ♠ A 10 3
                    ♥ A 8 5
                    ♦ K 6 5
                    ♣ A 10 7 3
```

West	North	East	South
–	–	–	1NT (15–17)
Pass	3NT	End	

West leads the ♠4 against 3NT and you hold up the ace until the third round, to break the link between the two defenders. What next?

You have seven top tricks and must establish the diamond suit in order to bump your total to nine. What is more, you cannot afford West to gain the lead or he will cash two more spade tricks, beating the contract. You will therefore play diamonds in the 'normal' way. You will cash the ♦K and then finesse the ♦J. As it happens, the finesse loses. You do not mind this at all because the safe (East) hand gains the lead and he has no spade to return. If he did have a spade left, the suit would break 4–4 and pose no threat to the contract.

Now let's switch a few cards, so that it is East who cannot be allowed to gain the lead:

```
              ♠ 7 6
              ♥ K 9 6
              ♦ A J 8 7 2
              ♣ K 6 5
♠ A J 9 4 2          N          ♠ 10 8 5
♥ Q 7 2                         ♥ J 10 4 3
♦ 10 9 4     W         E        ♦ Q 3
♣ J 4                 S         ♣ Q 9 8 2
              ♠ K Q 3
              ♥ A 8 5
              ♦ K 6 5
              ♣ A 10 7 3
```

West	North	East	South
–	–	–	1NT (15–17)
Pass	3NT	End	

West leads the ♠4 against 3NT and East plays the ♠10. You win with the ♠Q and note that you have seven top tricks, as before. How should you play the diamond suit?

If you make the same play as before, cashing the ♦K and finessing the ♦J, you will go down. East, who is now the danger hand because he can lead through your ♠K-3, will gain the lead. A spade return will then sink the contract.

You do better to cash the ace and king of diamonds. As the cards lie, the ♦Q will fall doubleton and you will score an overtrick. If the ♦Q does not fall, you will lead towards the ♦J on the third round. You don't mind at all if West began with ♦Q-10-4 and wins a diamond trick. West cannot continue spades effectively from his side of the table. If he plays any other suit, you will have the four diamond tricks that you need to bring your total to nine.

(The very best play, in fact, is to lead the ♦2 from dummy. If the ♦3 or ♦4 appears from East, you can cover with the ♦5. You would then succeed when West holds ♦10-9 doubleton, also when East carelessly plays low from something like ♦Q-9-4.)

Safety plays in the trump suit

Suppose you have a trump suit of ♠A-7-6-2 opposite ♠K-J-5-4. The best play of this suit, without regard for the whole deal, is to cash the ♠A and then to finesse the ♠J. You will score all four tricks when the ♠Q is onside and the suit breaks 3–2.

In the context of a complete deal, however, this may be quite the wrong play to make. Here is a deal that illustrates the situation:

```
                    ♠ A J 5 4
                    ♥ 10 7
                    ♦ A 9 3
                    ♣ A Q J 2
   ♠ 10 8                          ♠ Q 9 3
   ♥ K Q J 3          N            ♥ 9 6 5 2
   ♦ J 8 4        W       E        ♦ 10 7 2
   ♣ 9 8 6 5          S            ♣ 10 7 4
                    ♠ K 7 6 2
                    ♥ A 8 4
                    ♦ K Q 6 5
                    ♣ K 3
```

West	North	East	South
–	–	–	1NT (15–17)
Pass	2♣	Pass	2♠
Pass	6♠	End	

West leads the ♥K against your small slam in spades and you win with the ♥A. How will you play the contract?

Suppose you had overbid to a grand slam and therefore needed to pick up the trump suit without loss. You would make the normal play in the suit, cashing the king and then finessing dummy's jack. Here, though, you can afford to lose a trump trick provided you do not also lose a heart trick. You can see what will happen if you finesse the ♠J on the first or second round. East will win with the ♠Q and the defenders will cash a heart trick to beat the slam.

A better idea is to combine the second-best play in the trump suit (playing the king and the ace) with the chance that you can discard your two heart losers on dummy's clubs. After winning the heart lead, you cash the two top trumps. The ♠Q does not fall but both defenders follow. You then turn to the club suit. All follow to the first three rounds and you discard one of your heart losers. You then lead dummy's last club winner. It makes no difference whether West decides to ruff with his master ♠Q. You will discard your last heart anyway and make the slam.

Do you see why this was a good line of play? You had less chance of avoiding a loser in the trump suit, yes, but when the first chance (two top trumps) failed, you had a substantial second chance remaining – that you could discard your heart losers. The sum of these two chances was much higher than that offered by taking a trump finesse.

Let's stick with the same trump holding and see a quite different situation where you would deviate from the normal (finessing) line of play. On this deal you are worried about the defenders scoring a ruff against you:

```
              ♠ A J 5 4
              ♥ 9 7 6 4
              ♦ K 9 3
              ♣ K 4
♠ 10 9 3                      ♠ Q 8
♥ 3              N            ♥ K J 10 8 5 2
♦ 8 6 4      W     E          ♦ 10 7 2
♣ 10 9 7 6 5 2     S          ♣ J 8
              ♠ K 7 6 2
              ♥ A Q
              ♦ A Q J 5
              ♣ A Q 3
```

West	North	East	South
–	–	2♥	Dble
Pass	3♥	Pass	3♠
Pass	4♣	Pass	6♠
End			

East opens with a weak two-bid (see Chapter 5). You double for take-out and partner shows a strong hand with a cue-bid (see Chapter 10). When the spade fit comes to light, you bid a small slam. How should you play this when West leads the ♥3 to East's ♥K and your ♥A?

The bidding has told you that hearts are breaking 1–6. Suppose you play trumps in the normal way, cashing the ♠K and finessing the ♠J. There is a risk that East will win with the ♠Q and give his partner a heart ruff to defeat the slam. Not what you want! You should therefore play the ace and king of trumps, making sure that East does not gain the lead with a doubleton trump queen. As it happens, the ♠Q will fall and you will end with an overtrick. Suppose, though, that West had started with ♠Q-x-x or ♠Q-x-x-x. You would still make the contract, since you could lead towards the ♠J on the third round of the suit.

Once again, the second-best play in the trump suit, looking at it isolation, gives you the best chance of making the contract. And that is the important thing!

Points to remember

- When comparing two possible ways of playing a combination in a single suit, count how many different defensive holdings can be picked up by each line of play. Choose the way that will succeed against the greatest number of holdings.
- The correct way to play a suit often varies according to how many tricks you need from it.
- Sometimes it is not good enough to look only at the suit in question. You must consider the whole deal, particularly what may happen if a particular defender gains the lead. When one defender is a 'danger hand', you must do everything you can to prevent him from gaining the lead.
- When you hold eight or nine trumps between the hands and are missing the queen, it is not always enough to apply the 'eight ever, nine never' rule as to whether you finesse or play for the drop. Sometimes you must ignore the rule, to keep a dangerous defender off lead. You may choose to ignore it also when a ruff is threatened.

Test yourself

(1)

```
                      ♠ A 9 6 2
                      ♥ 2
                      ♦ A K 7 5 3
                      ♣ A Q 2
♦8 led       ┌─────────────┐
             │      N      │
             │  W       E  │
             │      S      │
             └─────────────┘
                      ♠ Q J 10 7 4
                      ♥ A K 7
                      ♦ Q J 2
                      ♣ K 9
```

West	North	East	South
–	1♦	Pass	1♠
Pass	4♠	Pass	4NT
Pass	5♣	Pass	6♠
End			

West leads the ♦8 against your small slam in spades. How will you plan the play?

(2)

```
                      ♠ A Q 3
                      ♥ K 9 2
                      ♦ Q 7 4 2
                      ♣ K 5 2
♠J led       ┌─────────────┐
             │      N      │
             │  W       E  │
             │      S      │
             └─────────────┘
                      ♠ K 7 6 4
                      ♥ A 7 3
                      ♦ A 6 3
                      ♣ A 8 6
```

West	North	East	South
–	–	–	1NT (15–17)
Pass	3NT	End	

West leads the ♠J against your contract of 3NT.

a How will you play the contract?
b How would you play 3NT if dummy's clubs were ♣10-5-2 instead?

Answers

(1)

          ♠ A 9 6 2
          ♥ 2
          ♦ A K 7 5 3
          ♣ A Q 2

♠ 8 3   ♠ K 5
♥ Q 9 8 6 4   N   ♥ J 10 5 3
♦ 8   W   E   ♦ 10 9 6 4
♣ J 8 5 4 3   S   ♣ 10 7 6

          ♠ Q J 10 7 4
          ♥ A K 7
          ♦ Q J 2
          ♣ K 9

West	North	East	South
–	1♦	Pass	1♠
Pass	4♠	Pass	4NT
Pass	5♣	Pass	6♠
End			

West leads the ♦8 against your small slam in spades. How will you plan the play?

If you had overbid to a contract of 7♠, you would make the 'normal' play in the spade suit, running the ♠Q. That's because you could not afford to lose a trump trick and finessing against the king is very much better than trying to drop a singleton king offside. Since you are in the more sensible contract of 6♠, you can afford a trump loser. What you cannot afford is to lose a diamond ruff as well. West's lead in dummy's main suit is very suspicious and the odds are high that the ♦8 is a singleton. What can you do about it?

The answer is that you should not take a trump finesse. Instead, you should play ace and another trump. East will take a trick with the ♠K, but since West has no trumps left the defenders cannot then score a diamond ruff. You don't mind at all if West began with ♠K-x or ♠K-x-x. He is welcome to score a trick with the ♠K because you cannot then lose a diamond ruff in addition. All that will be lost is a potential overtrick. It is worth giving up a few 30-point overtricks in order to make slams that would otherwise have gone down!

(2)

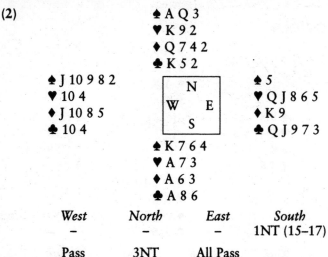

	West	North	East	South
	–	–	–	1NT (15–17)
	Pass	3NT	All Pass	

West leads the ♠J against your contract of 3NT. You have eight top tricks and therefore need only one more trick from the diamond suit (a total of two diamond tricks) to give you the contract. In other words, you must look for a safety play for two diamond tricks. Can you see it?

After winning the first spade trick, in either hand, you should cash the ♦A and then duck a round of diamonds. When the cards lie as in the diagram, the ♦K will fall from East and you will have the two diamond tricks that you need. If the ♦K does not fall, you will win the defenders' return and lead towards the ♦Q on the third round, still making the contract when West holds the ♦K or the diamond suit breaks 3–3.

Suppose next you were in the same contract but dummy's clubs were only ♣10-5-2. With just seven top tricks now, you would need three diamond tricks to give you the game. You would therefore make the 'normal' play in diamonds, ace first and then low to the queen. When West held ♦K-x-x, you would score the required three diamond tricks and make the contract.

16

destroying declarer's communications

In this chapter you will learn:

- how to give count signals when declarer plays a suit
- how to hold up an ace or king to kill a suit in dummy
- when to hold up with two stoppers
- how to remove an entry to dummy.

Holding up an ace in defence

When declarer is playing in a no-trump contract, he will often hold up the ace of the suit you have led. What is the purpose of this? To exhaust the holding of one of the defenders, so there will be no communication between the defenders' hands. Exactly the same situation can arise the other way round. A defender can hold up an ace to break the communications between declarer and the dummy. Let's see an example of that:

```
              ♠ 6 5 2
              ♥ 9 6
              ♦ 8 3 2
              ♣ K Q 10 7 3
♠ 9 7                          ♠ J 10 8 4
♥ Q J 8 4 2      N             ♥ K 7 3
♦ Q 10 7 4    W     E          ♦ J 9 5
♣ 9 4            S             ♣ A 8 5
              ♠ A K Q 3
              ♥ A 10 5
              ♦ A K 6
              ♣ J 6 2
```

West	North	East	South
–	–	–	2NT
Pass	3NT	End	

You are sitting East, defending 3NT, and partner leads the ♥4 to your ♥K. What does declarer do on this trick? Yes, he holds up the ace, aiming to break the communications between you and your partner. He ducks again when you return the ♥7. Declarer wins the third round of hearts and leads a club to the king. How will you defend?

Declarer has already given you a big hint with his own hold-up! You must play low, allowing dummy's ♣K to win. When declarer continues with a second round of clubs, you hold up again. You have restricted declarer to just two club tricks (rather than the four he would have scored if you had taken your ♣A too early). It will be pointless for him to play another round of clubs because he will then have no entry to dummy, to enjoy the two established cards in the suit. At this stage declarer has eight top tricks (three spades, one heart, two diamonds and two clubs). His only realistic chance of a ninth trick is that spades will break 3–3. Not today! Your hold-up of the ♣A will therefore defeat the contract.

Giving count signals

One point was glossed over in the description of that last 3NT contract. Can you think what it was? East needed to hold up his ♣A until the third round because declarer held three clubs. (If East had taken the ace on the second round, declarer would still have a club left and could cross to the dummy to score three more club tricks.) What if declarer had held only two clubs in his hand? Sitting East, you would then want to take your ♣A on the second round. If, instead, you were to duck, you would give declarer an undeserved second club trick, which might sometimes be enough for him to make the contract.

Let's change the last deal, giving South just two clubs (and making the spades 3–3):

```
                    ♠ 6 5 2
                    ♥ 9 6
                    ♦ 8 3 2
                    ♣ K Q 10 7 3
  ♠ 9 7 4                             ♠ J 10 8
  ♥ Q J 8 4 2      ┌─────────┐        ♥ K 7 3
  ♦ Q 4            │    N    │        ♦ J 10 9 5
  ♣ 9 4 2          │  W   E  │        ♣ A 8 5
                   │    S    │
                   └─────────┘
                    ♠ A K Q 3
                    ♥ A 10 5
                    ♦ A K 7 6
                    ♣ J 6
```

West	North	East	South
–	–	–	2NT
Pass	3NT	End	

Again declarer holds up the ♥A until the third round. As before, he then plays a club to the king, which you duck, and continues with a low club from dummy. What will happen if you hold up again, which was necessary on the previous version of the deal? Declarer will make the contract! He will have eight top tricks and the 3–3 break in spades will give him a ninth trick.

On this deal declarer holds only two clubs, so you must take your ♣A on the second round. How can you possibly know how many clubs declarer holds? There is only one way. Your partner (West) must tell you how many clubs he has. West will do this by playing high–low with an even number of clubs and low–high with an odd number of clubs. This is known as 'giving a count signal'.

When declarer holds only two clubs (♣J-6), your partner will hold ♣9-4-2. With three clubs, an odd number, he will signal with his lowest club (the ♣2) on the first round. If partner holds three clubs, declarer has only two and you should take your ♣A on the second round. The only other possibility is that partner holds a singleton club and declarer has four cards in the suit. Then it will not matter when you take your ace. So, on the version of the deal where declarer held two clubs, you would take your ace on the second round and beat the contract.

Now look back a couple of pages to the original version of the deal, where declarer held three clubs. Your partner would then play the ♣9 on the first round, his higher card, to show a doubleton. Placing declarer with three clubs (or four if partner has a singleton), you would hold up your ♣A until the third round and again beat the contract.

Great, isn't it? By playing count signals when declarer leads a suit like this, you will know how to defend all the time!

Most bridge players use attitude signals (high to encourage, low to discourage) when partner leads a suit. They use count signals (high to show an even number of cards, low to show an odd number) when declarer leads a suit.

Holding up a king in defence

Even when you hold the king of dummy's long suit, rather than the ace, you may be able to kill declarer's communications. Let's see an example of that:

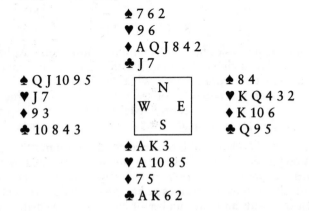

```
              ♠ 7 6 2
              ♥ 9 6
              ♦ A Q J 8 4 2
              ♣ J 7
♠ Q J 10 9 5              ♠ 8 4
♥ J 7          N         ♥ K Q 4 3 2
♦ 9 3      W     E       ♦ K 10 6
♣ 10 8 4 3     S         ♣ Q 9 5
              ♠ A K 3
              ♥ A 10 8 5
              ♦ 7 5
              ♣ A K 6 2
```

West	North	East	South
–	–	–	1♣
Pass	1♦	Pass	2NT
Pass	3NT	End	

You are sitting East and your partner leads the ♠Q against 3NT. Declarer wins with the ♠K and leads the ♦5 to West's ♦9 and dummy's ♦Q. How will you defend?

Suppose you win with the ♦K, returning a spade. Declarer will win with the ♠A and make an overtrick. He still has an entry to dummy, so he will score five diamond tricks. What could you have done about it?

West's ♦9 is a count signal and suggests that he may hold two diamonds, leaving declarer with two cards in the suit. You should hold up your ♦K, allowing dummy's ♦Q to win. Declarer cannot now score more than two diamond tricks and will go down in his contract. Indeed, if you duck smoothly declarer may return to his hand with the ♣A to repeat the diamond finesse. This time it will lose and he will then make only one diamond trick!

When the suit length is in declarer's hand, hidden from view, it can be more difficult to hold up a king. Take the East cards on this deal:

```
                    ♠ 8 2
                    ♥ A 8 4 3
                    ♦ A K Q 7
                    ♣ A Q 2
    ♠ K J 9 7 6            N          ♠ Q 5 4
    ♥ K 10 7 2       W         E      ♥ Q 9 6
    ♦ 10 2                            ♦ J 9 8 5
    ♣ 10 7                 S          ♣ K 9 6
                    ♠ A 10 3
                    ♥ J 5
                    ♦ 6 4 3
                    ♣ J 8 5 4 3
```

West	North	East	South
–	1♦	Pass	1NT
Pass	3NT	End	

West leads the ♠7 against 3NT and your queen wins the first trick. You persist with the ♠5, partner winning South's ♠10 with the ♠J. West then clears the spade suit, declarer winning with the ace. At Trick 4 declarer leads the ♣3, covered by West's 10 and dummy's queen. What is your plan for the defence?

Your first task is to read the lie of the club suit. Partner has played the ♣10. What does that mean? It indicates that he has either a doubleton ♣10-x or a singleton. He cannot hold ♣J-10 doubleton, or he would have played the jack. So, declarer is marked with five (or six) clubs to the jack. You must not release your king of clubs!

Suppose you are playing on auto-pilot and capture dummy's ♣Q with the king. Declarer will win your return and score four club tricks and three diamond tricks, to go with the major-suit aces. Instead, you should allow dummy's ♣Q to win. Declarer will no doubt continue with ♣A, hoping that the ♣K will fall. No such luck on this occasion and he will go two down. If he establishes the club suit, by playing a third round, he will have no way to reach the long cards in his own hand.

Holding up in defence with two stoppers

When dummy has one side entry, it may work well to hold up when you have two stoppers in dummy's long suit. Take the East cards on this deal:

```
              ♠ K 9 4
              ♥ 9 8 3
              ♦ K J 10 9 5
              ♣ 8 6
  ♠ Q 2                        ♠ J 10 8 5
  ♥ Q 10 7 2       N           ♥ J 6 4
  ♦ 8 4 2       W     E        ♦ A Q 6
  ♣ Q 9 7 2        S           ♣ J 10 3
              ♠ A 7 6 3
              ♥ A K 5
              ♦ 7 3
              ♣ A K 5 4
```

West	North	East	South
West	*North*	*East*	*South*
–	–	–	1♣
Pass	1♦	Pass	2NT
Pass	3NT	End	

West leads the ♥2 against 3NT and your ♥J is won by South's ♥K. Declarer continues with a diamond to dummy's jack, West signalling count with the ♦2. How will you defend?

It may seem natural to win with the ♦Q. Suppose you do this, returning the ♥6. Declarer will win with the ♥A and lead his last diamond to dummy, establishing the suit. It will do you no good to hold up the ♦A now, because the ♠K will be an entry to dummy. The defenders will score two hearts and two diamonds, but declarer will claim the remaining tricks. He will score three diamond tricks to go with his three ace-king combinations.

To kill dummy's diamond suit, you must duck on the first round, allowing the ♦J to win. When you capture the second round of diamonds, declarer will have no card left in the suit. If he uses the ♠K to reach dummy and set up the diamond suit, he cannot return to dummy to enjoy the established cards in the suit.

You would make exactly the same play if dummy held ♦Q-J-10-9-x and you held ♦A-K-x in defence. You would hold up on the first round so that declarer had no diamond remaining when you captured the second round.

Suppose instead that this was the lie of the diamond suit:

North
♦ Q J 10 9 5

West　　　　　　　　　　　*East*
♦ A 8 2　　　　　　　　　　♦ K 6 3

South
♦ 7 4

The diamond stoppers are divided between the two defenders' hands. The principle is exactly the same, however. When dummy contains a side entry in a different suit, neither defender must win the first round of diamonds. If East wins the first round with the ♦K, for example, declarer will have a diamond left in his hand and will be able to clear the suit.

Removing an entry to dummy

When dummy holds a long suit accompanied by one side-suit entry, the defenders' top priority may be to remove this entry. Suppose you had been East on the following deal. Would you have defended correctly?

```
                    ♠ A
                    ♥ 9 8 3
                    ♦ K Q J 10 7 5
                    ♣ 8 6 2
  ♠ 10 7 6 4                        ♠ J 8 5 2
  ♥ Q 10 7 2          N            ♥ A 6 4
  ♦ 8 2          W        E        ♦ A 6 3
  ♣ Q 10 7           S             ♣ J 9 3
                    ♠ K Q 9 3
                    ♥ K J 5
                    ♦ 9 4
                    ♣ A K 5 4
```

West	North	East	South
–	–	–	1♣
Pass	1♦	Pass	1NT
Pass	3NT	End	

Your partner, West, leads the ♥2 and you win with the ♥A. What should you do next?

There are two possible guidelines to follow at this stage. One is 'always return your partner's suit'; another is the recommendation posted on the office walls of one of the world's top computer companies: 'THINK!'

Suppose you do return a heart. Declarer, who knows from the ♥2 lead that hearts are breaking 4–3, will rise with the ♥K. He will then establish the diamond suit. It will do you no good to hold up the ♦A for a round or two because the ♠A is still available as an entry. The defenders will take three heart tricks and one diamond. Declarer will then score the remaining tricks to make his contract.

Instead of returning partner's suit, you should play a spade to remove the ♠A entry to dummy. You can then hold up the ♦A for one round (West would have led a spade from a five-card suit, so South's likely shape is 4–3–2–4). You win the second round of diamonds and continue hearts, West winning and clearing the suit. Declarer will have only seven top tricks. He can establish an eighth trick, in the club suit, but that will still be one down.

Points to remember

- When you hold the ace of a long suit in the dummy, you should generally hold up until the round that will exhaust declarer's holding in the suit (the second round, for example, if declarer holds two cards). Partner will give you a count signal, allowing you to determine how many cards declarer has in the suit.
- Similarly, you may be able to kill a long suit in dummy (or sometimes in declarer's hand) by holding up a king.
- Even when you hold two stoppers in dummy's suit, it can be right to hold up on the first round. This is the case when declarer holds a doubleton and dummy has one side-entry in a different suit.
- When dummy contains a threatening side suit that will soon be established, see if you can kill the suit by removing a potential entry card.

Test yourself

(1)

```
                    ♠ Q
                    ♥ 10 8 5
                    ♦ Q J 10 7 3
                    ♣ 9 8 4 3
   ♠10 led          ┌─────────┐      ♠ K 5 4 2
                    │    N    │      ♥ Q 10 9 6
                    │ W     E │      ♦ A 6 4
                    │    S    │      ♣ 6 5
                    └─────────┘
```

West	North	East	South
–	–	–	2NT
Pass	3NT	End	

You are sitting East and West leads the ♠10, covered by the queen, king and South's ace. Declarer continues with the ♦K and (if this is allowed to win) the ♦2. How will you defend if West follows with the ♦5 and the ♦8? How would you defend if West follows instead with the ♦8 and then the ♦5?

(2)

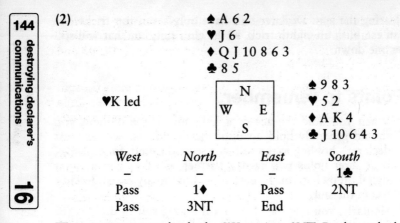

♠ A 6 2
♥ J 6
♦ Q J 10 8 6 3
♣ 8 5

♥K led

N
W E
S

♠ 9 8 3
♥ 5 2
♦ A K 4
♣ J 10 6 4 3

West	North	East	South
–	–	–	1♣
Pass	1♦	Pass	2NT
Pass	3NT	End	

West, your partner, leads the ♥K against 3NT. Declarer ducks the first trick and West continues with the ♥Q, which is also allowed to win. When West plays the ♥10, dummy discards a club and you throw a low spade. Declarer wins with the ♥A and leads the ♦9, West following with the ♦7. What is your plan for the defence?

Answers

(1)

♠ Q
♥ 8 5 2
♦ Q J 10 7 3
♣ 9 8 4 3

♠ 10 9 8 7 3
♥ A 7
♦ 9 8 5
♣ 10 7 2

N
W E
S

♠ K 5 4 2
♥ Q 10 9 6
♦ A 6 4
♣ 6 5

♠ A J 6
♥ K J 4 3
♦ K 2
♣ A K Q J

West	North	East	South
–	–	–	2NT
Pass	3NT	End	

West leads the ♠10 against 3NT and, sitting East, you cover dummy's ♠Q with the ♠K. Declarer wins with the ♠A and plays the ♦K, West signalling his count with the ♦5. Since declarer must hold at least two diamonds for his 2NT opening, it is clear that you should hold up your ♦A on the first round. At Trick 3, declarer continues with the ♦2, your partner playing the ♦8 and dummy playing the ♦Q. What now?

West has shown three diamonds by playing low–high in the suit. This leaves declarer with only two diamonds and you should therefore win the second round of the suit. You return a spade and declarer has no way to make the contract.

On this deal it was essential for you to take the ♦A at exactly the right moment. Suppose you had ducked the ace for a second time. Declarer would then have eight top tricks available and could have set up a ninth by leading a heart from dummy to his jack.

Next, suppose that the cards lie differently and your partner signals high–low in diamonds, playing the ♦8 followed by the ♦5. When partner holds two diamonds, declarer will hold three. So you would hold up the ♦A until the third round, restricting declarer to two diamond tricks instead of four.

(2)

```
                    ♠ A 6 2
                    ♥ J 6
                    ♦ Q J 10 8 6 3
                    ♣ 8 5
  ♠ J 10 7 4                         ♠ 9 8 3
  ♥ K Q 10 9 4        N              ♥ 5 2
  ♦ 7 2           W       E          ♦ A K 4
  ♣ 9 7               S              ♣ J 10 6 4 3
                    ♠ K Q 5
                    ♥ A 8 7 3
                    ♦ 9 5
                    ♣ A K Q 2
```

West	North	East	South
–	–	–	1♣
Pass	1♦	Pass	2NT
Pass	3NT	End	

West, your partner, leads the ♥K against 3NT. Declarer ducks the first trick and West continues with the ♥Q, which is also allowed to win. When West plays the ♥10, dummy discards a club and you throw a low spade. Declarer wins with the ♥A and leads the ♦9, West following with the ♦7. What is your plan for the defence?

If you win the first round of diamonds, declarer will win your black-suit return in the South hand and clear the diamond suit. The defenders will score just two hearts and two diamonds and declarer will make the contract.

To defeat 3NT you must hold up on the first round of diamonds, even though you hold two stoppers in the suit. The contract will then go one down. By holding up in this way, you restrict declarer to just one diamond trick.

7

two-suited overcalls

In this chapter you will learn:
- the Unusual No-trump overcall
- the Unusual No-trump over a minor suit
- how to respond to the Unusual No-trump
- Michaels cue-bids
- how to respond to a Michaels cue-bid
- the 2NT response to Michaels.

The Unusual No-trump

Suppose your right-hand opponent opens 1♠ and you overcall 2NT. What should such a bid mean? Without any discussion, you might assume that it showed a balanced hand with good spade stopper – a hand that was a few points stronger than a 1NT overcall, perhaps around 19–21 points. That's fair enough, but many years ago players realized that you could launch a strong balanced hand with a take-out double, rebidding some number of no-trumps later. They invented a new meaning for a jump overcall of 2NT. It would show at least five cards in both of the minor suits. This convention is standard in tournament bridge and widely used in rubber bridge too. It is known as the Unusual No-trump, usually abbreviated to UNT.

Suppose you are second to speak and the player in front of you has opened 1♠ (or 1♥). You have to find a bid on one of these hands:

a ♠ 6	b ♠ J 2	c ♠ 6
♥ 9 4	♥ 3	♥ 2
♦ A Q J 8 7	♦ K 9 7 6 2	♦ K Q J 10 2
♣ K J 10 5 2	♣ Q 10 8 5 3	♣ A K J 10 7 2

Hand **a** is perfect for the UNT. Both your suits are well-packed with honours and you would be very unlucky to go for a big penalty at the three-level. Hand **b** is not so suitable and most players would not venture 2NT, even when non-vulnerable against vulnerable. Hand **c** is super-strong. You would start with 2NT and bid again over partner's response, to let him know that you held an unusually strong hand and there might be a chance of game. (Over a 3♦ response, you would rebid 4♣ to tell him that your clubs were longer.)

When you bid 2NT you are naturally hoping that your side may end up playing the contract with one of the minor suits as trumps. However, another important objective is that you are taking a lot of bidding space away from the opponents. The player to your left, for example, will no longer be able to respond 2♥ to 1♠, or to raise 1♠ to 2♠. So, 2NT can be useful in two ways. It can help you bid constructively on a hand with the minor suits (you could not double on such a hand because of your shortage in the other major). You can also interfere seriously with the opponents' bidding.

Unusual No-trump over a minor suit

When the opponents have opened with a one-bid in a minor suit, you can use 2NT to show the lowest two unbid suits. So, over 1♣ a 2NT overcall would show hearts and diamonds. Over 1♦, it would show heart and clubs.

Responding to the Unusual No-trump

How do you respond when partner overcalls 2NT? Most of the time, you will simply bid three of your better minor. Remember that an 11-trick game in a minor suit requires considerable values. When you have a particularly good fit, you can bid one of the minors at the four-level or the five-level.

Particularly when non-vulnerable, you may jump to 5♣ or 5♦ on a hand with a big trump fit but limited general values. Your intention will be to make life difficult for the opponents, who will doubtless hold a great fit in one of the major suits. Bear the vulnerability in mind at all times. When partner is vulnerable, he will have a reasonable hand to venture a 2NT overcall.

Suppose the opponents only are vulnerable and the bidding starts like this:

West	North	East	South
1♥	2NT	Pass	?

What would you respond on the following South hands?

a ♠ Q 8 3 2   b ♠ K 9 4   c ♠ A 10 6 5 4
  ♥ A Q 6 4   ♥ Q 10 8 6 5 2   ♥ 2
  ♦ Q 8 7   ♦ 8 7   ♦ K J 9 7 2
  ♣ 9 5   ♣ 10 2   ♣ K 3

On hand **a** you respond at the minimum level, bidding 3♦. It is unlikely that you can make a game and you must choose the response that will be right most of the time. With **b** you were not at all happy to hear partner's UNT. Don't make this obvious to the world by frowning (or, heaven forbid, muttering 'That's very awkward')! Bid 3♣ straight away and let the opponents worry what to do. Hand **c** represents a fantastic fit for partner. You should go all the way to 5♦. If the opponents double, thinking that you have bid high in an effort to shut them out, they may end up being disappointed when your partner makes the contract.

Bidding 2NT after two passes

Until now we have been discussing a 2NT overcall by the player sitting over the opening bidder. What should 2NT mean in an auction like this?

West	North	East	South
1♥	Pass	Pass	2NT

Some players give 2NT the same meaning as in the second seat; it is the Unusual No-trump. The majority of players prefer the bid to be natural, though, showing around 18–20 points, perhaps bolstered by one long minor suit. So, if you start playing the Unusual No-trump you must discuss with your partner whether it applies also in the fourth seat, after two passes.

The Michaels cue-bid

You will realize by now that tournament players do not like to leave any bid without a meaning! Suppose your right-hand opponent opens 1♣. What do you think an overcall of 2♣ should mean?

Many decades ago, an overcall in the opponents' suit showed a very strong hand of some sort. This was a complete waste of the bid, since you can launch such hands with a take-out double, bidding strongly thereafter. So, tournament players prefer to use a cue-bid in the opponents' suit to show a two-suited hand of at least 5–5 shape. This is the scheme:

2♣ over 1♣	shows both major suits
2♦ over 1♦	shows both major suits
2♥ over 1♥	shows spades and one of the minors
2♠ over 1♠	shows hearts and one of the minors

Known as the Michaels cue-bid, the bid shows as many major suits as is possible – both of them over a minor-suit opening, the other major over a major-suit opening. The point-count of the hand may be quite modest, about the same as for a one-level overcall. That's because there is more chance of outbidding the opponents when you hold the major suits. Suppose your right-hand opponent has opened 1♣ and you have to find a bid on one of these hands:

a	♠ K J 8 4 2	b	♠ A Q 10 9 5	c	♠ J 9 7 6 2
	♥ K 10 9 6 4		♥ K Q J 8 2		♥ 10 8 6 4 3
	♦ 7		♦ A 2		♦ K J
	♣ 9 5		♣ 8		♣ A

Hand **a** is fine for a non-vulnerable 2♣ overcall. When vulnerable, many players would pass, since their partner would expect a slightly stronger hand. Hand **b** is considerably stronger. You would begin with 2♣ and then raise partner's 2♥ or 2♠ response to the three-level to invite game. Hand **c** is not particularly suitable, because 8 of the 9 points lie in the short suits. Nevertheless, some players would venture a non-vulnerable Michaels cue-bid. At least they would interrupt the opponents' auction.

When you make a major-suit Michaels bid, particularly 2♠ over 1♠, the bidding is likely to be carried higher than after a minor-suit Michaels bid. Your hand should be correspondingly stronger, to avoid conceding a sizable penalty at the three-level. Suppose your right-hand opponent has opened 1♠ and you hold one of these hands:

a	♠ 4 2	b	♠ 5	c	♠ 2
	♥ A 9 8 6 4		♥ K Q J 8 2		♥ K Q 10 8 7 2
	♦ A Q 7 4 2		♦ 7 2		♦ A J 8 7 2
	♣ 10		♣ A Q 10 8 2		♣ 5

Hand **a** contains two moderate suits and you might go for a large penalty at the three-level if you found partner with an unsuitable hand. Some players might risk a 2♠ Michaels bid when non-vulnerable, but this would not be a sound bid. It would simply be a gamble that you would find partner with some sort of fit and disrupt the enemy auction. It is best to pass on such a hand.

Hand **b** is more like it! You hold two good suits and a perfect hand for a 2♠ overcall. On hand **c**, with a good six-card heart suit, you should overcall 2♥. If partner has two hearts and three diamonds, you don't really want to play in diamonds rather than hearts. Apart from that, you are more likely to reach a playable 4♥ if you emphasize your good hearts.

Responding to a Michaels cue-bid

When partner has made a Michaels cue-bid, you should assume that he has a minimum for his bid and respond accordingly. It is similar to responding to a take-out double. If you have a good fit, or a strong hand, you can show your strength by jumping. Suppose the bidding starts like this:

West	North	East	South
1♦	2♦	Pass	?

... and you have to find a response on one of these South hands:

a ♠ 9 7
  ♥ Q 10
  ♦ A 7 2
  ♣ K J 9 6 4

b ♠ K 10 8 7 2
  ♥ Q 4
  ♦ A 9 8 2
  ♣ 10 7

c ♠ 9 2
  ♥ 8
  ♦ J 10 7 2
  ♣ A Q 9 8 6 3

On hand **a** you should respond just 2♥. Remember that partner may hold a modest hand of around 8 points or so. If he has a singleton club, for example, he will not find your club holding very useful. Hand **b** represents a fantastic fit for spades and you should leap all the way to 4♠. Even opposite a minimum Michaels overcall you expect to have a reasonable play for game. On hand **c** you bid 2♠, responding at the minimum level in your better major. It's not your fault that you don't have three-card support for one of partner's suits.

When partner has made a major-suit Michaels bid and you want to play in his minor suit, you respond 3♣:

West	East	West	North	East	South
♠ Q 3	♠ J 9 7 4	–	–	–	1♠
♥ A Q 10 5 4	♥ K 3	2♠	Pass	3♣	Pass
♦ K J 10 6 2	♦ Q 9 8 3	3♦	End		
♣ 3	♣ J 10 5				

West's 2♠ overcall shows at least 5–5 shape in hearts and an unspecified minor. East sees that he will have a fit in partner's minor suit, whichever one it is. He responds 3♣, which West will pass if his minor suit is clubs. Here West's second suit is diamonds, so he corrects to 3♦, which becomes the final contract.

The 2NT response to Michaels 2♥/2♠

Just occasionally you will hold a very strong hand in response to a Michaels overcall in a major suit. In that situation you may wish to find out more about partner's hand in order to bid the best contract. You respond 2NT, which asks partner to describe his hand further. Suppose the bidding starts:

West	North	East	South
1♥	2♥	Pass	2NT
Pass	?		

South has asked partner to describe his hand further. North rebids according to this schedule:

3♣ Lower-range hand with spades and clubs
3♦ Lower-range hand with spades and diamonds
3♥ Upper-range hand with spades and clubs
3♠ Upper-range hand with spades and diamonds

A lower-range hand would be around 8–13 points. Upper-range would be 14+ points. On some hands, the responder might pass a rebid of 3♣ or 3♦. Facing an upper-range rebid, he would probably bid game in one of the overcaller's suits.

Points to remember

- In the second seat (sitting to the left of the opening bidder), you can bid 2NT to show a hand that is at least 5–5 in the minor suits. This convention is known as the Unusual No-trump.

- Most players use 2NT in the fourth seat (after a start such as 1♥ – Pass – Pass) to show a strong balanced hand. If you want to treat 2NT as the Unusual No-trump in the fourth seat, you should agree this with your partner.

- In both the second and fourth seats, a cue-bid in the enemy suit (such as 2♣ over 1♣) is a Michaels cue-bid. A cue-bid in a minor suit shows both the major suits. A cue-bid in a major suit shows the other major and an unspecified minor. The overall strength may be moderate, particularly when non-vulnerable.

- After a major-suit Michaels cue-bid (such as 1♥ – 2♥), responder may bid 3♣ to say that he wants to play in three of partner's minor suit.

- After a major-suit Michaels cue-bid, responder may bid 2NT to ask for more information about the overcaller's hand. With a lower-range overcall, partner rebids 3♣ or 3♦ to show his minor. With an upper-range hand, he will rebid 3♥ (with clubs) or 3♠ (with diamonds).

Test yourself

(1) The bidding starts like this:

West	North	East	South
1♥	?		

What would you say on the following North hands?

a ♠ –	b ♠ A Q 8	c ♠ A Q 10 7 6
♥ 10 2	♥ A J 10 6	♥ 7
♦ Q J 10 8 3 2	♦ K 9 4	♦ 8 2
♣ K Q J 9 4	♣ A Q 3	♣ A 10 9 7 4

(2) What will you respond on the following South hands when, at Love All, your partner makes an UNT overcall?

West	North	East	South
1♠	2NT	Pass	?

a ♠ A 10 8 6 5 2	b ♠ K Q 9 6 4	c ♠ A 9 8 5 2
♥ 8 2	♥ Q 10 8 7 3	♥ 9
♦ Q 10 8	♦ 6	♦ 7 2
♣ 4 2	♣ J 7	♣ A Q J 8 2

(3) What will you respond on the following South hands when, at Love All, your partner makes a Michaels cue-bid?

West	North	East	South
1♥	2♥	Pass	?

a ♠ A 10 8 6	b ♠ 4	c ♠ A 9 2
♥ A 8	♥ Q 10 8 7 3	♥ 9
♦ K 10 7 3	♦ J 10 7 6	♦ A Q 8 6 3
♣ K 9 4	♣ A 8 3	♣ A 10 8 4

Answers

(1) **a** 2NT. Perfect for an Unusual No-trump overcall. You have two sound suits, offering you every protection against a big penalty.

  b Double. With a flat 20-count, you start with a double. 2NT would show the minors, remember.

  c 2♥. Perfect for a Michaels cue-bid.

(2) **a** 3♦. Partner has shown at least five cards in both minors. You choose diamonds because you have better support for diamonds than for clubs.

  b 3♣. You prefer clubs to diamonds. It is not your fault that you don't have better support.

  c 5♣. With such excellent club support, there is a good chance that you can make game.

(3) **a** 4♠. Even if partner has quite a modest Michaels cue-bid, you should have a good play for game.

  b 3♣. You want to play in partner's minor suit at the three-level. If partner holds spades and diamonds, he will bid 3♦ now.

  c 2NT. Make the special relay bid to discover which minor suit partner holds. You can then raise to game in that suit.

18

counting the hand

In this chapter you will learn:
- how to count the defenders' hands
- how to use the information gained.

One of the most important techniques in bridge is an apparently simple one – counting. It may seem easy but it takes discipline to force yourself to do it, hand after hand. What should you count? As declarer you need to count the shape of the defenders' hands. Once you know how many cards a defender holds in each suit, the play will become very much easier. You can also count high-card points. If someone opened a 15–17 point 1NT and has already shown up with 16 points outside clubs, you will know that he cannot hold the ♣Q. Finally, you can count tricks. Particularly in defence, it is important to count the tricks that you need to beat the contract. Suppose you are defending 3NT, for example, and can see three certain tricks. You must look for two more from some quarter.

In this chapter we will look at counting shape and the benefits that can flow from the knowledge that you gain.

Counting to assist a two-way guess

When a contract depends on a two-way guess for a queen, don't rush to take this decision. Play on the other suits and try to determine which defender holds more cards in the key suit. The player with the greater number of cards will be favourite to hold the missing queen. Deals such as the following are commonplace:

```
                    ♠ 9 4 2
                    ♥ A 9 5
                    ♦ A K 5
                    ♣ K J 6 3
   ♠ A K J 10 6                      ♠ 8 3
   ♥ 8 6            ┌─────────┐      ♥ 10 4 2
   ♦ J 9            │    N    │      ♦ Q 10 7 6 4 2
   ♣ Q 9 7 4        │ W     E │      ♣ 8 2
                    │    S    │
                    └─────────┘
                    ♠ Q 7 5
                    ♥ K Q J 7 3
                    ♦ 8 3
                    ♣ A 10 5
```

West	North	East	South
–	–	–	1♥
1♠	2♠	Pass	3♥
Pass	4♥	End	

North's 2♠ shows a sound heart raise and game in hearts is duly reached. West leads the ♠A and receives an encouraging ♠8 from his partner. He continues with king and another spade, East ruffing the third round. East switches to a trump and you draw trumps in two more rounds. How will you continue?

You have lost three tricks already and the contract depends on you guessing which defender holds the ♣Q. If you think East holds the missing queen, you will finesse the ♣10. If, instead, you think West holds the card, you will finesse the ♣J. Which defender is more likely to hold the ♣Q, do you think?

The bidding provides little clue, because West has already shown enough strength to merit a one-level overcall. The defender who holds more clubs than his partner will be favourite to hold the queen of the suit. At the moment West has shown up with seven cards in the majors and East began with only five. So, East is currently the favourite to hold the ♣Q.

Instead of playing on clubs immediately, you cash the ace and king of diamonds and ruff a diamond. You now have a 'complete count of the hand'. West started with a 5–2–2–4 shape. He has four clubs to East's two and is therefore twice as likely as East to hold the ♣Q. You cash the ♣A and finesse dummy's ♣J. On this occasion justice is done. West does indeed hold the missing ♣Q and you make the contract.

Sometimes you can be certain that a finesse will work:

```
              ♠ A Q 2
              ♥ A J 5
              ♦ A K 9 3
              ♣ K J 3
♠ J 10 5 3       N        ♠ 7 6 4
♥ 9 8 6       W     E     ♥ 10 7 4 2
♦ 2              S        ♦ J 8 6 4
♣ 10 9 8 6 4              ♣ 7 2
              ♠ K 9 8
              ♥ K Q 3
              ♦ Q 10 7 5
              ♣ A Q 5
```

West	North	East	South
–	–	–	1NT (15–17)
Pass	7NT	End	

West leads the ♣10 against 7NT. How will you play the contract?

You have 12 tricks on top and can make a thirteenth trick from the diamonds, provided the suit breaks 3–2 or you guess correctly which defender holds ♦J-x-x-x. (If it is East, you will need to cash the ace and king first; if it is West, you will need to cash the ace and queen.) You should aim to get an accurate count on the spades, hearts and clubs before guessing which honours to cash first in the diamond suit.

You win the club lead and cash two more rounds of clubs. East shows out on the third round, so you have a count on that suit. When you continue with three rounds of spades and three rounds of hearts, both defenders follow all the way. West has shown up with at least 11 cards in spades, hearts and clubs. He cannot possibly hold four diamonds! So, you cash the ace and king of diamonds, knowing for sure that this is the right thing to do. West shows out on the second round of diamonds, and you finesse the ♦10, making the grand slam.

Suppose, instead, that West had shown out on the third round of both spades and hearts. His shape would then be 2-2-4-5 and you would play the diamond suit differently, cashing the ace of diamonds and then the queen. A finesse of dummy's ♦9 would then land the grand slam.

When an opponent has made a pre-emptive bid it is often quite easy to obtain a count on the hand. Would you have kept track of the suit lengths on the next deal?

```
              ♠ 4 3
              ♥ A 8 5
              ♦ A K 6
              ♣ A 10 6 5 3
♠ K Q J 8 6 2        N        ♠ A 9 5
♥ J 6 3                       ♥ 9 7 2
♦ 9 8 5      W         E      ♦ 7
♣ 4                  S        ♣ K Q J 9 8 2
              ♠ 10 7
              ♥ K Q 10 4
              ♦ Q J 10 4 3 2
              ♣ 7
```

West	North	East	South
2♠	Dble	4♠	5♦
End			

West opens with a weak two-bid, showing six spades and around 6–10 points. North doubles for take-out and East raises pre-emptively to 4♠. Your bid of 5♦ ends the auction and the defenders cash two rounds of spades, West then switching to a trump. How will you play the contract?

The only problem is a potential loser on the fourth round of hearts. If clubs break 4–3, you can set up a long club for a heart discard and avoid the need to take any guess on the third round of hearts. You win the trump switch with the ♦10, cross to the ♣A and ruff a club with the ♦Q. Unfortunately, West shows out on this trick. What now?

Since there is no future in setting up the clubs, you might as well draw trumps. You play a trump to dummy's ace and East shows out. Have you been keeping a count of the hand? West started with six spades, shown in the bidding, and has since shown up with one club and three diamonds. So, his shape is 6–3–3–1 and the hearts are breaking evenly!

You draw West's last trump and play the three top heart honours. As if by magic, West's ♥J does indeed fall on the third round and you make the contract.

Suppose, instead, that West had turned up with two clubs, making his shape 6–2–3–2. You would then have drawn trumps, cashed the king and ace of hearts and finessed the ♥10 on the third round of the suit. You can see how useful it is to obtain a complete count on the deal. Many a time it will save you from a difficult guess in a side suit.

Points to remember

- When you have a two-way queen guess, play on the other suits first and aim to get a 'complete count on the hand'. The defender who started with more cards in the key suit is more likely to hold the missing queen.
- Many hands become easier to play if you keep track of how many cards each defender holds in each suit.

Test yourself

(1)

                  ♠ Q 5
                  ♥ Q 9 6 2
                  ♦ A Q 4
                  ♣ A 7 4 2

♠K led

```
        N
    W       E
        S
```

                  ♠ 4
                  ♥ A K J 10 3
                  ♦ K J 5
                  ♣ K Q 9 6

West	North	East	South
3♠	Pass	Pass	4♥
Pass	5♥	Pass	6♥
End			

How will you play the small slam when West leads the ♠K –
East signalling count with the ♠2 – and continues with the ♠A?

(2)

                  ♠ Q 9 5
                  ♥ Q J 6 2
                  ♦ Q J 4
                  ♣ A 10 4

♥10 led

```
        N
    W       E
        S
```

                  ♠ A K 3
                  ♥ A K 4
                  ♦ K 8 5 3
                  ♣ K J 6

West	North	East	South
–	–	–	2NT
Pass	4NT	Pass	6NT
End			

West leads the ♥10 and you win with the ♥A. How will you play
the small slam?

Answers

(1)

```
                        ♠ Q 5
                        ♥ Q 9 6 2
                        ♦ A Q 4
                        ♣ A 7 4 2
   ♠ A K J 10 7 6 3          ┌─────────┐          ♠ 9 8 2
   ♥ 7 4                     │    N    │          ♥ 8 5
   ♦ 8 6 3                   │ W     E │          ♦ 10 9 7 2
   ♣ 5                       │    S    │          ♣ J 10 8 3
                             └─────────┘
                        ♠ 4
                        ♥ A K J 10 3
                        ♦ K J 5
                        ♣ K Q 9 6
```

West	North	East	South
3♠	Pass	Pass	4♥
Pass	5♥	Pass	6♥
End			

North's 5♥ asked partner to bid a slam if he held a control (ace, king, singleton or void) in the enemy spade suit. How would you play the small slam when West leads the ♠K – East signalling count with the ♠2 – and continues with the ♠A?

You draw trumps in two rounds and all now depends on bringing in the club suit without loss. Whenever you have a potential key guess to make in a suit, it may help you to play the other side suits first. Your aim is to obtain a complete count of the hand. When you play three rounds of diamonds, important information comes to light. West follows all the way. That marks his shape as 7–2–3–1 (or possibly 7–2–4–0). Since West can hold at most one club, you cash the ♣A on the first round. Two lowly spot cards appear and you know, from your count of the hand, that East has ♣J-10-8 remaining. You lead a low club from dummy and, when East produces the ♣8, you finesse the ♣9. West shows out (surprise, surprise!) and the slam is yours.

It would do East no good to play the ♣J or ♣10 on the second round, of course, because you would win and return to dummy to finesse the ♣9 on the third round. Indeed, it would be poor defence for East to play one of his honours. By playing low instead, he would beat the slam whenever declarer had been too lazy to count the hand and was about to play the clubs from the top!

(2)

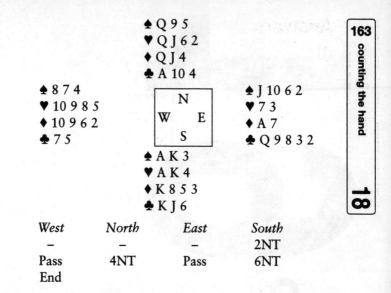

♠ Q 9 5
♥ Q J 6 2
♦ Q J 4
♣ A 10 4

♠ 8 7 4
♥ 10 9 8 5
♦ 10 9 6 2
♣ 7 5

♠ J 10 6 2
♥ 7 3
♦ A 7
♣ Q 9 8 3 2

♠ A K 3
♥ A K 4
♦ K 8 5 3
♣ K J 6

West	North	East	South
–	–	–	2NT
Pass	4NT	Pass	6NT
End			

North's 4NT is a non-forcing limit bid that invites a slam. You decide to bid 6NT and West leads the ♥10, which you win with the ♥A. How will you play the contract?

Once you have forced out the ♦A you will have 11 top tricks. Unless you can score four diamond tricks, you will need to guess which defender holds the ♣Q. What is the best way to play the diamonds?

If the diamond suit breaks 3–3, all will be easy. You should lead twice towards dummy's ♦Q-J-4, which will also allow you to score three diamond tricks when West has a doubleton ♦A. As it happens, East wins the ♦Q with the ♦A and returns a heart. When you test the diamond suit, East discards a club on the third round. You now need to guess the club suit correctly. The defender who began with the majority of clubs will be favourite to hold the missing ♣Q and you must therefore play the other suits, aiming to build up a count on the hand.

Both defenders follow to three rounds of spades and when you play dummy's last two heart winners, East shows out on the third round and discards one spade and another club. You have a complete count on the hand. East began with 4–2–2–5 shape. The odds are therefore '5-to-2 on' that East was dealt the ♣Q. You cash dummy's ♣A and, at Trick 12, finesse the ♣J. Justice is served on this occasion. The finesse succeeds and the slam is yours.

9

duplicate bridge

In this chapter you will learn:
- how duplicate bridge is played
- how to use bidding boxes
- how to alert a conventional bid
- how a duplicate pairs event is scored.

What is duplicate bridge?

Perhaps you have never played duplicate bridge, in a club, and are wondering whether to undertake such an adventure. In this final chapter of the book, we will look at the differences between a home game of rubber bridge and a duplicate pairs session.

First of all, what does the term 'duplicate bridge' mean? It means that every hand will be played more than once, in an attempt to reduce the luck factor. Your own score on each deal will be compared with other pairs who have played exactly the same cards as you. If you score better than they do, you will have a 'good board'; if they score better, you will have a 'poor board'. We will look at the scoring method in a moment. What actually happens when you and your partner arrive at the club?

You will be assigned a 'pair number' and an initial 'seating position'. For example, the organizer may tell you that you are Pair 11 and will start as North–South at Table 3. You go to those positions and play begins. On the first round of the event, you will probably have to deal the cards for each board. You bid and play the hand, as at rubber bridge, but instead of gathering the four cards at the end of each trick, you play all 13 of your cards in a line in front of you. If you win a trick, you place the card lengthways, pointing at your partner. If the other side wins a trick, you place it sideways, pointing towards your opponents. So at any stage, you can easily see how many tricks you have won and lost.

When the deal is completed, each player returns his 13 cards to a plastic or wooden container, known as a board. This contains four slots marked 'North', 'East', 'South' and 'West'. In this way the deal is preserved and other contestants can play it later. The board also contains a 'travelling score-sheet', on which the contract and result will be marked. The entry for the board you have just played may, for example, look like:

N–S pair	E–W pair	Contract	Played by	N–S	E–W
11	4	4♠ + 1	S	650	

This would indicate that, as North–South, Pair 11 made one overtrick in Four Spades and scored +650. When you are vulnerable (this will be marked on the board itself) the game bonus is 500. So the score of 650 is made up of five major-suit tricks at 30 points each, plus the vulnerable game bonus. A non-vulnerable game bonus is 300 and a part-score bonus is worth 50. The first time you play, the other contestants will assist you with the scoring. North is the player responsible for filling in the score-sheet.

A typical 'round', played against the same opponents, will consist of two, three or four boards. The organizer will then call 'Move, please!' and you may then have to move to another table. A 'movement card' on the table will tell you where your next move is. It may say, for example, 'Go to East–West, Table 6'.

Bidding boxes

In most clubs you will make your bids and calls via the cards in a 'bidding box', rather than by word of mouth. If you want to bid 2♦, you put your thumb on the 2♦ bidding card and lift it, together with all the cards behind it (which represent the bids lower than 2♦), placing it on the table in front of you. Should you make another bid, Pass, Double or Redouble later, you will place the bidding card or cards on top of the 2♦ card, offset to the right. In this way the calls displayed in front of you will represent all the calls that you have made. Your line might, for example, be:

| 2♦ | 3NT | Pass |

Your partner, who we will say, opened the bidding with 1♠, might have a line of calls like this:

| 1♠ | 2♠ | 4♠ |

If the opponents passed throughout, they will each have a line of green Pass cards before them. So, everyone can see that the bidding was:

West	North	East	South
–	1♠	Pass	2♦
Pass	2♠	Pass	3NT
Pass	4♠	End	

Calling the director

If any potential infraction of the Laws arises, the players should call the director. He or she will then come to the table and make a 'ruling', possibly after referring to the relevant section of the Rule Book. For example, the director should be called if a revoke occurs.

Alerting conventional bids

When your partner makes a bid that is conventional in your agreed system, you should say 'Alert!' or wave the blue Alert card from the bidding box. The opponents then have the right to ask what the bid meant. For example, if you open 1NT and partner responds 2♦, which is a transfer bid indicating hearts, you should wave the Alert card.

How is the scoring done?

In a duplicate pairs event, the scoring is done at the end of the session. Your score on each board will be compared with that of each other pair in your direction who played the board. You will score 2 matchpoints for each pair that you managed to beat and 1 matchpoint for each pair with whom you tied. Suppose four other pairs played the board, you beat two of them and tied with another. You would score 2 + 2 + 1 = 5 matchpoints out of a possible 'top' of 8 matchpoints.

A score-sheet for a board in a five-table event might look like this:

			Score		Matchpoints	
N-S pair	E-W pair	Contract	N-S	E-W	N-S	E-W
1	6	4♥ + 1	650		5	3
2	9	4♥ + 2	680		8	0
3	7	6♥ –1		100	2	6
4	8	4♥ + 1	650		5	3
5	10	6♥ x –1		200	0	8

Pair 2 obtained a 'complete top' in the North–South direction, scoring 8 matchpoints for making two overtricks in Four Hearts. Pair 5 obtained a 'bottom' in the North–South direction, going one down doubled in Six Hearts (the 'x' represents a doubled contract) and scoring minus 200 and 0 matchpoints.

As you see, overtricks are much more important in a Pairs event than in rubber bridge. If you make ten tricks in 3NT, you beat all the pairs who managed to score only nine tricks. You get two matchpoints for each pair that you beat, whether the margin is just 30 or several hundred. So, in a Pairs event you may sometimes put your contract at risk, searching for a valuable overtrick. It is an important part of this form of the game, to judge what risks are worth taking.

The pair with the highest total of matchpoints for all the boards will win the session. In some clubs the scoring will be completed soon after the play is over. (If you have had an awful session, you may hurry home saying, 'I won't wait for the results!'). In other clubs, the scoring may be done the next day and you can either phone the organizer to see how you did, or wait until the following week to look at the posted results sheet.

Why should I play duplicate bridge?

Playing duplicate bridge is the best way to improve your game. By comparing your results with the other pairs, you can tell whether you did well on a board or not. This is not so easy to judge in rubber bridge, where you can win a session merely because you happened to be dealt very good cards.

Most bridge clubs are registered with the national bridge organization of the country. They will award 'master points' to those who do well in each event (usually the top third or top quarter of the field). By collecting these over your lifetime you can attain various levels, such as Local Master, County Master, even perhaps the exalted title of Lifemaster or Grandmaster.

We have reached the end of the book and the time has come for me to wish you good luck in the game – whatever your ambitions may be!

teach yourself®

From Advanced Sudoku to Zulu, you'll find everything you need in the **teach yourself** range, in books, on CD and on DVD.

Visit **www.teachyourself.co.uk** for more details.

Advanced Sudoku & Kakuro	Beginner's Dutch
Afrikaans	Beginner's French
Alexander Technique	Beginner's German
Algebra	Beginner's Greek
Ancient Greek	Beginner's Greek Script
Applied Psychology	Beginner's Hindi
Arabic	Beginner's Italian
Aromatherapy	Beginner's Japanese
Art History	Beginner's Japanese Script
Astrology	Beginner's Latin
Astronomy	Beginner's Portuguese
AutoCAD 2004	Beginner's Russian
AutoCAD 2007	Beginner's Russian Script
Ayurveda	Beginner's Spanish
Baby Massage and Yoga	Beginner's Turkish
Baby Signing	Beginner's Urdu Script
Baby Sleep	Bengali
Bach Flower Remedies	Better Bridge
Backgammon	Better Chess
Ballroom Dancing	Better Driving
Basic Accounting	Better Handwriting
Basic Computer Skills	Biblical Hebrew
Basic Mathematics	Biology
Beauty	Birdwatching
Beekeeping	Blogging
Beginner's Arabic Script	Body Language
Beginner's Chinese	Book Keeping
Beginner's Chinese Script	Brazilian Portuguese

Bridge
Buddhism
Bulgarian
Business Chinese
Business French
Business Japanese
Business Plans
Business Spanish
Business Studies
Buying a Home in France
Buying a Home in Italy
Buying a Home in Portugal
Buying a Home in Spain
C++
Calculus
Calligraphy
Cantonese
Car Buying and Maintenance
Card Games
Catalan
Chess
Chi Kung
Chinese Medicine
Chinese
Christianity
Classical Music
Coaching
Collecting
Computing for the Over 50s
Consulting
Copywriting
Correct English
Counselling
Creative Writing
Cricket
Croatian
Crystal Healing
CVs
Czech
Danish
Decluttering
Desktop Publishing
Detox
Digital Photography
Digital Home Movie Making

Dog Training
Drawing
Dream Interpretation
Dutch
Dutch Conversation
Dutch Dictionary
Dutch Grammar
Eastern Philosophy
Electronics
English as a Foreign Language
English for International
   Business
English Grammar
English Grammar as a Foreign
   Language
English Vocabulary
Entrepreneurship
Estonian
Ethics
Excel 2003
Feng Shui
Film Making
Film Studies
Finance for Non-Financial
   Managers
Finnish
Fitness
Flash 8
Flash MX
Flexible Working
Flirting
Flower Arranging
Franchising
French
French Conversation
French Dictionary
French Grammar
French Phrasebook
French Starter Kit
French Verbs
French Vocabulary
Freud
Gaelic
Gardening
Genetics

Managing Your Own Career
Mandarin Chinese Conversation
Marketing
Marx
Massage
Mathematics
Meditation
Modern China
Modern Hebrew
Modern Persian
Mosaics
Music Theory
Mussolini's Italy
Nazi Germany
Negotiating
Nepali
New Testament Greek
NLP
Norwegian
Norwegian Conversation
Old English
One-Day French
One-Day French – the DVD
One-Day German
One-Day Greek
One-Day Italian
One-Day Portuguese
One-Day Spanish
One-Day Spanish – the DVD
Origami
Owning a Cat
Owning a Horse
Panjabi
PC Networking for Small
  Businesses
Personal Safety and Self
  Defence
Philosophy
Philosophy of Mind
Philosophy of Religion
Photography
Photoshop
PHP with MySQL
Physics
Piano

Pilates
Planning Your Wedding
Polish
Polish Conversation
Politics
Portuguese
Portuguese Conversation
Portuguese Grammar
Portuguese Phrasebook
Postmodernism
Pottery
PowerPoint 2003
PR
Project Management
Psychology
Quick Fix French Grammar
Quick Fix German Grammar
Quick Fix Italian Grammar
Quick Fix Spanish Grammar
Quick Fix: Access 2002
Quick Fix: Excel 2000
Quick Fix: Excel 2002
Quick Fix: HTML
Quick Fix: Windows XP
Quick Fix: Word
Quilting
Recruitment
Reflexology
Reiki
Relaxation
Retaining Staff
Romanian
Running Your Own Business
Russian
Russian Conversation
Russian Grammar
Sage Line 50
Sanskrit
Screenwriting
Serbian
Setting Up a Small Business
Shorthand Pitman 2000
Sikhism
Singing
Slovene

Small Business Accounting
Small Business Health Check
Songwriting
Spanish
Spanish Conversation
Spanish Dictionary
Spanish Grammar
Spanish Phrasebook
Spanish Starter Kit
Spanish Verbs
Spanish Vocabulary
Speaking On Special Occasions
Speed Reading
Stalin's Russia
Stand Up Comedy
Statistics
Stop Smoking
Sudoku
Swahili
Swahili Dictionary
Swedish
Swedish Conversation
Tagalog
Tai Chi
Tantric Sex
Tap Dancing
Teaching English as a Foreign
  Language
Teams & Team Working
Thai
The British Empire
The British Monarchy from
  Henry VIII
The Cold War
The First World War
The History of Ireland
The Internet
The Kama Sutra
The Middle East Since 1945
The Second World War
Theatre
Time Management
Tracing Your Family History
Training
Travel Writing

Trigonometry
Turkish
Turkish Conversation
Twentieth Century USA
Typing
Ukrainian
Understanding Tax for Small
  Businesses
Understanding Terrorism
Urdu
Vietnamese
Visual Basic
Volcanoes
Watercolour Painting
Weight Control through Diet &
  Exercise
Welsh
Welsh Dictionary
Welsh Grammar
Wills & Probate
Windows XP
Wine Tasting
Winning at Job Interviews
Word 2003
World Cultures: China
World Cultures: England
World Cultures: Germany
World Cultures: Italy
World Cultures: Japan
World Cultures: Portugal
World Cultures: Russia
World Cultures: Spain
World Cultures: Wales
World Faiths
Writing a Novel
Writing Crime Fiction
Writing for Children
Writing for Magazines
Writing Poetry
Xhosa
Yiddish
Yoga
Zen
Zulu